To
Alastair

Best wishes

Enjoy!

Barry Brown

June 2010.

Stars In My Eyes

A Movie & Media Memoir

Barry Brown

authorHOUSE®

AuthorHouse™ UK Ltd.
500 Avebury Boulevard
Central Milton Keynes, MK9 2BE
www.authorhouse.co.uk
Phone: 08001974150

First published by AuthorHouse 12/17/2009

ISBN: 978-1-4490-5696-4 (sc)

This book is printed on acid-free paper.

For Amanda and Dugald

Acknowledgements

I wrote the first draft of this book in 1998. I did no research and have never kept a diary but I have a good memory. All inaccuracies, errors and omissions are therefore my fault. At first it was a longer and more rambling memoir but with hindsight and the help of family and friends it is now a more manageable length. My former BBC colleague Genevieve Eckenstein at the behest of another friend Joy Whitby made the first editing task painless and helpful.

The sociologist Dr. Robert Bocock suggested a fresh beginning for the narrative, based on a work experience rather than the more conventional chronological introduction. An American economist friend, Avis Waring made creative and grammatical improvements in 2002, and more recently, encouraged me to prepare this final draft. It is she who suggested self-publishing the book, knowing that my life story had languished for years in manuscript form.

For the past 10 years I have lectured on film history on cruise ships, embellishing my film profiles with personal anecdotes and reminiscences. My thanks go to the hundreds of passengers who have asked if I have published my memoirs. At last here is their chance to read them. For 'oldie' non-travellers, I trust it will be a nostalgic trip down memory lane.

At first the book was called *NameDropper,* a word which can sometimes be perceived as derogatory. As the text is full of name-dropping on my part, I could think of no other title. I am therefore grateful to my son Dugald for suggesting *Stars in my Eyes* which is more appealing – and just as accurate. He is also responsible for finding the relevant art work for the front cover, which he so cleverly designed.

My sincere thanks go to Jill Talbot who is a wizard with the electronic management of photographs. It was she who scanned, cropped and collated the 8 pages of photographs, then added the captions. It is a magical task which I can hardly comprehend. My thanks, too, to Linda Davies for her stalwart dissection of the clip-art work for the front cover.

This memoir is also a description of life in the media of bygone times, so different from today. I hope it will provide an insight into the history of communication both in the UK and abroad, especially those who are interested in film and media studies, whether at school, college or University.

Most of all, I hope I have managed to remind readers of many movie stars from the vintage years who deserve to be remembered by all generations for many generations to come.

Finally my thanks go to the production team at *Authorhouse* who have been so professional in guiding me through the complex process of modern online publishing.

Barry Brown
London
October 2009

Contents

One   Starstruck

It was a black tie dinner and everyone was seated by 7pm when the Prince of Wales arrived. Guests at the top table included two great cinema directors who were to receive a prestigious award. One was Orson Welles, a larger-than-life overweight 68 year-old who had stunned the world in 1941 at the age of 26 with an astonishing piece of well-crafted movie-making *Citizen Kane*, now a cinema classic.

The other director could not have been more different. He was Marcel Carne, a short, bald, diffident Frenchman of 80 who had also stunned movie audiences in 1944 with *Les Enfants du Paradis*, also a cinema classic.

The Guildhall, the elegant 15th century building in the City of London, not far from St. Paul's Cathedral, was an unlikely venue for luminaries from the 20th century movie industry to gather in September 1983. But gather they did to celebrate the 50th Anniversary of the British Film Institute. The event was considered so important that BBC2 had planned a 'live' transmission hosted by the journalist and broadcaster Barry Norman right on the dot of 9pm. Outside Broadcast vans and trails of coaxial cable were hidden from view as the 700 guests arrived.

Several BBC TV executives and producers were among those present and the seating plan created some uneasy pairings. The Controller of BBC2, Brian Wenham, urbane, brilliant and easily bored was placed next to the British movie star Anna Neagle, then in her late seventies who had played such heroines as Nell Gwynn, Nurse Edith Cavill, Odette and Queen Victoria. They hardly spoke.

At a nearby table the BBC producer Alan Yentob who had recently made an *Arena* profile of Orson Welles, was seated next to Orson Welles' elderly but spry personal assistant. Another BBC Producer sat opposite and all three chatted amiably whilst a four course dinner was served by an army-drilled bevy of unobtrusive waitresses. Coffee had been served just as the 'live' broadcast began.

The precision timing of the meal was more impressive than the BBC broadcast. Prince Charles spoke, the audience applauded, Barry Norman rounded off the programme and the dining crowd dispersed to other parts of the building.

Orson Welles held court in a small room to anyone who cared to listen; Marcel Carne walked aimlessly like a benign bank manager at a cocktail party; Prince Charles was secreted to a special area with BFI governors and movie personnel. It was out-of- bounds to those not deemed appropriate to meet the royal personage. The Boulting Brothers, identical twins John and Roy, had produced and directed a series of films pillorying national institutions - *I'm All Right Jack, Brothers in Law, Private's Progress* to name but a few. They were too subversive to be invited into the inner sanctum, but when the young BBC Assistant Producer who had worked on the telecast, collapsed whilst chatting to them, they did all they could to comfort him and seek medical assistance. The poor chap was OK after a while, simply overwrought. He could not have been looked after by two kinder gentlemen.

Eventually people began walking more freely in and out of the royal enclosure so the BBC TV Producer wandered in. He was about to approach the actor/film director Richard Attenborough, the current BFI Chairman, when TV presenter Barry Norman walked in. He had noticed that his BBC colleague had joined the celebrity throng so he decided to do the same.

One of the guests recognised Barry Norman from his regular appearances on BBC1 so walked over to talk to him. It was Prince Charles. He asked Barry what he thought of the much-heralded *The Draughtsman's Contract* which had been partly financed by the BFI. Barry was attempting to be as diplomatic as possible when suddenly someone tugged the base of Prince Charles' jacket. His Royal Highness swiftly turned to find the culprit. It was the legendary movie mogul Sam Spiegel who had produced *The African Queen, Bridge on the River Kwai* and *Lawrence of Arabia*. The burly bully simply wanted to introduce the Prince to his latest floozy. That was the end of Barry's brief meeting with the Prince of Wales.

How do I know this? I was that TV Producer standing beside him. Being Australian and more 'pushy' than my namesake, I had inadvertently gate-crashed a no-go area and met a Prince. But then I have always been star-struck. It started when I was four years old.

In 1934 my father took me to the Mayfair Theatre in my home city, Sydney to see my first movie. Why do I know it was called *One Night of Love* and starred Grace Moore? I just do. I was enthralled by the darkened palace and the enormous black-and-white faces of beautiful people looking down at me. All I remember about the film was that Grace Moore lived in a sumptuous house and sang. One day a doctor came and pricked her naked stomach with a pin. I laughed. From then on I was hooked on cinema.

Why did my parents in the Sydney suburb of Willoughby have varnished doors, not the same colour as the walls, like Grace Moore's house? Why did they have a black telephone when movie people had white ones? When we acquired a

piano it was dark wood veneer. Years later, when I bought
my own piano, it was white. Oh the power of Hollywood.
My need for glamour started at an early age.

Shirley Temple changed my life. She was only two years
older than I and she was famous. I wanted to be in movies
with her. She parachuted oh so bravely from an aeroplane,
she sang cheekily about the animal crackers in her soup
and she tap-danced superbly with a gangly black man.
For a time my affections drifted to the tomboy actress,
Jane Withers but not for long. Shirley was everywhere. In
newspapers and magazines we saw pictures of the house
20th Century Fox had built for her on the lot; we saw her
with her parents when she met President Roosevelt; we
saw newsreels of her birthday parties. There were cut-out
Shirley Temple books; there were Shirley Temple dolls; and
at school there was always one girl in class who had Shirley
Temple curls. I was sad when she grew up, married twice,
had a mastectomy and became a US Ambassador. Then she
wrote her autobiography, one of the best I have ever read, in
which she showed no animosity towards her parents, who
had unwisely invested her million dollar earnings and left
her almost broke. I loved her all over again.

I went every Saturday afternoon to my local Theatre Royal.
My somewhat snobbish mother gave my brother and me
nine pence each so that we could sit in the dress circle - it
was sixpence in the stalls and they had much more fun,
especially when the screen stars started kissing. They pelted
each other with peanuts, popcorn, whatever. We never did
that upstairs. And so I got to love William Powell and Myrna
Loy as Nick and Nora Charles in *The Thin Man* and, most of
all, their clever dog, Asta. He was white too, like the doors,
the telephones and the pianos.

As I travelled in the green and cream trams which clanked
round a sharp corner by the cinema, I was entranced by the
ever-changing posters announcing forthcoming features.
The poster for *The Good Earth* was the best. There was a

plague of some kind and there was a wonderful drawing of a Chinese woman called Luise Rainer! I was only seven years old but I remember she won the 1937 Best Actress Oscar for that film. <u>And</u> it was her second in a row - the previous year she had won it for *The Great Ziegfeld* - the first to achieve this. Then I never heard of her again.

Fifty years later I discovered she had been born in Germany, became a Hollywood actress and had married, first to the distinguished playwright Clifford Odets, then to a wealthy British publisher and lived in London with her priceless paintings and antique furniture. She had, apparently fallen foul of MGM's mogul, Louis B. Mayer, but she emerged from a 60 year retirement in 1996 to appear in a screen adaptation of the Dostoyevsky classic *The Gambler* in which she gave a scene-stealing performance. Then, during the 70th Anniversary Oscar ceremony in 1998, a tableau of previous winners was one of the highlights of the show. I watched it on TV and saw Luise Rainer once more, all 88 years of her. She still looked pretty. If you live long enough, Hollywood usually forgives.

The following year, 1938, came *Boys Town*. This was a different kind of Hollywood and I was glad to live with loving parents in sunny Sydney rather than be like poor, tough Mickey Rooney who had to stay with other delinquents in a home founded by Father Flanagan. He was a Roman Catholic priest. My Grandpa Forsyth, a staunch Methodist, hated Catholics. Perhaps they were different in America. Father Flanagan was really Spencer Tracy and like Luise Rainer, he won two Oscars in consecutive years, first for *Captain's Courageous* then *Boys Town*. I was storing this movie trivia in my mind and I was not yet ten years old. Truth to tell, I identified more closely with the goody-goody young star of *Captain's Courageous*, Freddie Bartholomew, but I wished I could be more like Mickey Rooney, cheeky and confident.

I also gained more movie knowledge from my daily visits to Mrs. Sutherland's shop. Outside the store were movie posters in lurid print of what was showing at the local picture house. I can still remember Cary Grant and Irene Dunne looking at each other in profile for a film with the beguiling title (for an eight-year-old) *The Awful Truth.* I thought, *how could truth be awful?*

I was thrilled when they advertised an Australian film *Dad and Dave Come to Town.* It was my favourite radio show and now I could see this family of country bumpkins in the flesh. Years later I realised that one of its young, wooden actors was the 21 year old Peter Finch who went on to win the first posthumous Best Actor Oscar in 1976 for *Network* in which he played a TV prophet, obviously insane, whose nightly rhetoric attracted millions. Little did I know then that one day I would produce a documentary about him for the BBC.

As a child, the one actress I could not abide was Bette Davis. She was neither beautiful nor amusing like Claudette Colbert and Katharine Hepburn. Her acting was strange (I later called it *mannered*) and she was always smoking. In one movie she had two cigarettes in her mouth. Later when I saw *Now Voyager* on TV, I treasured that poignant moment with Paul Henreid.

When I eventually met Bette Davis at BBC TV Centre in 1975 to record an interview with TV presenter Tony Bilbow for my weekly BBC2 production *Film Night,* I found her flirtatious, funny, but serious when talking about what she had achieved in her long film career.

She chuckled sexily as she explained how she had acquired her horrendous look as the demented, long-faded movie star Baby Jane Hudson in *Whatever Happened to Baby Jane.* She said that no make-up man would have taken credit for a face like that. She did it herself, lots of powder, too much mascara and a slash of bright red lipstick - in four minutes flat.

At the end of the recording I thanked her for her marvellous interview. In return she told me I had been *most professional*. My production team and I had really looked after her. She was a Hollywood legend and she appreciated the gesture. I was chuffed.

The next time I saw her was in 1988 on stage at the BBC TV Theatre on London's Shepherd's Bush Green after an appearance on the chat show *Wogan*. The interviewer, Terry Wogan, tried not to mention the new book she was plugging called *This & That*. As an Aries she would have none of that. She made sure it was mentioned and its cover shown - in close-up!

Miss Davis was dressed in a smart navy-blue-and-white suit with matching hat and veil. She smoked, using a long cigarette holder. It was only for effect, she never inhaled. She had had a stroke and a mastectomy and was painfully thin, her tiny legs like match sticks. Long after the studio audience had left, she sat on stage - she could not manage the steps up to the Green Room. There she autographed photos and books and chatted easily to the production team and me.

She had made her last film *The Whales of August* with another legend, Lillian Gish (I do not count the undecipherable *The Wicked Stepmother* which she left in a huff after a week's shooting), yet she continued to travel the world making public appearances when it was obvious she was not well.

In 1990 in a hotel on the outskirts of Paris, having been guest-of-honour at a minor Spanish film festival, she died - an ignominious end to a great screen actress. In the late 1930s I was too young to appreciate her in *Jezebel, Dark Victory, The Old Maid* and *The Private Lives of Elizabeth and Essex*. Thanks to TV I have been able to reassess her remarkable talent.

In 1968 my BBC colleague, Joan Bakewell, had been asked to interview Bette Davis on stage at London's National Film

Theatre. Joan told me how she had thought long and hard about how to introduce the actress to the packed audience. It was finally agreed that all she would say from the stage would be *Ladies and gentlemen, Miss Bette Davis*. The actress would enter from the back of the theatre and walk to the stage to tumultuous applause. This is exactly what happened. But Joan told me of her recurring nightmare before the event. In her dream she said, *Ladies and gentlemen, Miss Betty Grable*!

When I was nine I graduated from Hopalong Cassidy westerns to the adventures of Tarzan. At the time he was played by former Olympic swimming champion, Johnny Weissmuller. His Jane was Maureen O'Sullivan, later to become the mother of Mia Farrow, but I was more enchanted by Cheetah, Tarzan's ever-present chimpanzee. When I was ten I saw *Tarzan Finds A Son* which featured a young actor called Johnny Sheffield. He became my idol. He was my age. I wanted to *be* Johnny Sheffield, to be bold and brave in the jungle clad only in a loin cloth, with Cheetah as my best friend and strong Tarzan as my guide.

I met Johnny Weissmuller at London's Savoy Hotel in 1976 when he was promoting the MGM compilation movie *That's Entertainment 2*. He was then 72 and looked good for his age. He still had longish hair in the same swept-back style, only thinner. He was tall, not stooped and fairly trim, unless the bulky suit he was wearing hid a multitude of indulgence. I cannot imagine now why I did it, but I asked the ageing actor to repeat his famous Tarzan cry. What's more, he *did*, on an autumn day in one of London's poshest hotels! He hung around with the film crew long after his interview, which was unusual. Then the phone rang. It was Mrs. Weissmuller demanding his immediate return to their suite. Life in the jungle was much easier, poor man.

My father was a civil engineer and in April 1940 we left our suburban haven and went to live in Walgett, population 1000, in north-west New South Wales - the outback. The main street was made of red clay. Once during a drought I saw a camel stroll along it straight from the bush. Despite the myriad of items on sale at the General Store the camel kept walking. My favourite haunts were the Greek café (steak, chips and fried egg) and the local picture house.

In the year I lived there, before returning to my grandparents in Sydney to attend secondary school, I cannot remember one film I saw in Walgett. The blandness of the place - no changing coloured lights on the curtains, no Wurlitzer organ, no swirling staircase, no picture palace magic, must have affected me. I read about the Hollywood stars in my mother's *Australian Women's Weekly* and was fascinated by such glamorous names as Annabella (how chic to be known by one name), Greta Garbo, Tyrone Power and John, Lionel and Ethel Barrymore. Although I was known as Barry, I had been christened Barrymore. My mother insisted I was not named after the famous family. What a pity. There was only one thing her eldest son wanted to become - a film star. It was never to be, but as an adult I met many during my broadcasting career. I had stars in my eyes.

Two   Wilde About Cornel

As a fifteen year old my favourite film by far was the now little-known *A Song To Remember* about the composer Chopin and filmed in Technicolor. I saw it three times and remembered much of the dialogue. My favourite scene was when a rather ill Chopin was playing one of his compositions and on the keyboard in close-up, blood dropped from his nose. It is a real movie cliché but for me at Sydney's ornate State Theatre it was magical. I treasured that dramatic moment. If only *I* could create visual moments like that.

The real star of the film for me was Chopin's music. It gave me a life-long passion for classical music. It was the most exquisite music I had ever heard. I now realise that the Spanish pianist Jose Iturbi, who dubbed the music for the film, was not the world's best exponent of this romantic composer's work, but at the time I thought he played brilliantly. As a budding amateur pianist I rushed and bought an album containing pianoforte excerpts from the film. Fortunately they had been adapted and simplified which I did not know at the time, so I played these comparatively easy pieces over and over and over again.

Many film and music critics have been dismissive of the saccharine way in which classical music has been portrayed in the cinema but without *A Song To Remember* the tremendous impact of this kind of music on my life might not have occurred.

The star of the film was a newcomer (to me) by the name of Cornel Wilde. It was, in fact, his 10th screen appearance after earning a place in the USA's Olympic fencing team and acting for a time on the Broadway stage. He had played Louis Mendoza in Humphrey Bogart's 1941 movie *High Sierra* and was a passable Mexican. He had dark good looks, enormous brown eyes and curly black hair. To me he *was* Chopin although I remember he had a strange relationship with a manly woman called George Sand. I never believed in her because she was Merle Oberon and I had seen her in *Wuthering Heights*. For my money, I never enjoyed another Cornel Wilde film as much as *A Song To Remember*, not even when he played a trapeze artist in Cecil B. De Mille's spectacular *The Greatest Show on Earth*.

In the 1960s Cornel Wilde made a reputation for himself as an independent director and star of such ecological films as *The Naked Prey* and *Beach Red*. He was ahead of his time but I did not realise it then. In 1970 I eventually met him when I arranged for him to record a TV interview in London about his latest movie *No Blade of Grass*. It was about a virus destroying crops and causing such anarchy that one family took refuge in Britain's Lakes District. Cornel Wilde, by now in his mid-50s, was still a good-looking man, fit and well, but he wore plain, unfashionable clothes.

It was a thrill to meet this quietly spoken, unassuming man. The interview with the presenter Tony Bilbow began. It was slow and boring as Mr. Wilde struggled to find the right words to describe the reasons why he wanted to make this film. He was humourless and dull. His co-star was his wife, Jean Wallace, a truly awful actress. He must have loved her dearly because he mentioned her over and over again. In the control room I was getting desperate. Thank goodness it was a recording and not a 'live' performance. Normally, I recorded a 10 minute interview and transmitted it unedited, wherever possible, owing to the difficulties of handling videotape at that time. To salvage this interview I would need to record much more and edit it, no matter what.

After more than 20 minutes the desperate interviewer interrupted an interminable answer to his simple question and said, as customary, *Cornel Wilde, thank you*.

The actor protested *I haven't finished yet*.

Oh yes you have, responded the normally polite Tony Bilbow. I couldn't have agreed with him more. The interview was never transmitted. It wasn't worth editing. Although Cornel Wilde was the most boring Hollywood star I had encountered, I am sure he was a very nice man. I was sad when I read of his passing in 1989. He was the best Chopin I never knew.

Deanna Durbin was another favourite. Her ingenuous prettiness and amazing vocal talent wooed me at a very early age. From her I became aware of opera which, too, has become a lifelong interest. On stage at the end of her 1937 film *100 Men and a Girl* she asked the conductor if he knew *Traviata*. He turned to the orchestra, said *Traviata* and they started to play. Deanna, without any orchestral rehearsal, sang divinely. I now realise that she performed an Act I duet in Verdi's opera *La Traviata* - Hollywood decreed it would be a solo.

I was so impressed with dear Deanna. She sang in Italian and she was only 15! What a gal. She was one of the Hollywood stars I would love to have met but never did. This Canadian phenomenon retired from the screen at 27, married a Frenchman and went to live outside Paris. In the late 1970s I came in telephone contact with a BBC Radio 2 Producer, Sandra Black, who somehow had been able to visit the elusive Miss Durbin for a programme she was researching. She told me that Deanna had copies of all her movies but one, so I endeavoured to find a print of it for her, without success. That is the nearest I got to my second schoolboy screen crush - after Shirley Temple. The Hollywood producer of her movies, Joe Pasternak put it most succinctly when he said *she is one of those personalities whom the world will insist on regarding as its private property.* It was certainly true in my case.

Women singers in movies attracted me more than men. Tenors were OK, sometimes too short and dumpy. The only baritone I was aware of was Nelson Eddy. He was quite attractive but sopranos were much more glamorous - well, the ones in movies were. Grace Moore was the first, next came Deanna Durbin, then Jeanette MacDonald, who was pretty despite her long jaw. She had sparkling eyes and even more sparkling teeth. I winced at the extraordinary sound she made when she sang *Beyond the Blwooo Horizon,* but loved her duets with Nelson Eddy.

When Jeanette faded from the scene I followed the burgeoning career of Kathryn Grayson. She was petite and pretty but there was something about her voice which told me it was not great - there was too much vibrato - by now I had developed a more discerning ear. Kathryn's real name was Zelma Hedrick. I had not recognised her as one of Andy Hardy's dates in that popular 1940s movie series starring Mickey Rooney. I first noticed her in *Thousands Cheer* when I was fourteen. She played the daughter of an army officer who fell for Gene Kelly; but for me the pinnacle of her career was her singing *Make Believe* in the 1951 remake of Jerome Kern's *Show Boat.* Her curled dark hair, big brown eyes, red lipstick on her tiny mouth, big bosom and nipped in waist in a Southern belle's frilly dress, made her so attractive as she performed on the famous Mississippi river boat recreated in glorious Technicolor on the then large MGM back lot.

Exactly 25 years later I met Kathryn Grayson in London. She was then in her early 50s, overweight and wearing an oyster grey trouser suit. I was disappointed and I no longer have any idea how she answered the questions put to her by the interviewer, Barry Norman. All I remember is the moment when she showed me a picture of her mock Tudor house in Los Angeles and pointed out how the roof had been sprayed with asbestos to make it safe from local brush fires. Didn't she know about asbestosis which caused lung cancer? She also showed me the credit card she used at her local gas station. It was strange to see the name *Kathryn Grayson* emblazoned on it. I suppose it was better than *Zelma Hedrick*!

Three   Kaye Is For Danny

After World War II, Brisbane had a population of 800,000 and while everyone seemed to go to bed rather early, it had two cathedrals and was the capital of Queensland. This is where my family settled in 1946 after my father was discharged from the Royal Australian Air Force at the end of World War II.

Suburban cinemas there had to be experienced to be believed. They had canvas seats, rather like seaside deck chairs all joined together in rows, with a sloping concrete floor. They were cavernous and the sound echoed throughout the building. Whenever there was a boring bit, the younger teenagers rolled empty glass Coke and lemonade bottles down the floor towards the screen while the older ones canoodled in the back rows. Sometimes the noise was deafening and I cannot ever remember a cinema manager doing anything about it. Occasionally the adults would protest with *shushhhhh*, otherwise pandemonium reigned, unless the movie was either action-packed or very funny.

Abbott & Costello were popular and so was Danny Kaye, particularly with my brother Ron. I tolerated them but was not a big fan. The only line from a Danny Kaye film I remember is when he says to a shopkeeper *the trouble with you is the only exercise you get is jumping to conclusions.*

The party pieces written by Kaye's then wife, Sylvia Fine were something else altogether. I loved them. They were witty and funny. Only then could I marvel at Danny Kaye's comic mastery. I could tell that he was extremely musical - a talent I have always admired - and his face-pulling antics worked for me in this context. Who can forget that brilliant song dedicated to those arriving at the cinema half-way through a movie? You have to have lived at a time when there were continuous cinema screenings in order to appreciate its satirical message.

In a semi-tropical city like Brisbane, you often went to an air-conditioned cinema in the early evening just to get cool. I recall seeing the British comedian Tommy Trinder half-way through *Champagne Charlie,* staying until I reached the point where I had come in. What a way to see a movie? But it did not bother me one bit. What's more, Tommy Trinder was a talented British comedian with a long face and a broad grin which he used to great comic effect. His timing was impeccable in movies. Thirty-five years later in London, at a dinner in honour of the 80th birthday of the glamorous British screen actress and musical comedy star, Evelyn Laye, Tommy Trinder, who was 10 years her junior, provided the cabaret. His jokes were archaic and long-winded, his timing had gone to pot and he was just plain boring. The audience could not wait for him to finish. I wonder whether or not he sensed that. He didn't seem to.

To end the evening, the birthday "girl" herself, statuesque and elegant in a long, pale grey frock, graced the stage. She half-sang, half-talked her way through the Noel Coward's classic *I'll See You Again* from his musical *Bitter Sweet.* It was wonderful. But then all those years ago Mr Coward had written it especially for Miss Laye. If ever there was a star, it was she.

But back to Danny Kaye. The only reason I saw so many of his movies was because my brother liked him. I almost enjoyed *Wonder Man* and *The Secret Life of Walter Mitty* but I always wondered what he was like in real life. Was he a sad clown with a manic streak? Was he completely bonkers? He wasn't bad looking, he was talented, yet I didn't like him very much.

In the autumn of 1968 Danny Kaye was in London to promote his latest film *The Madwoman of Chaillot*. I took a BBC film crew to the Savoy Hotel. As a television producer/ director, I was only with these Hollywood stars for a couple of hours at most. Usually it gave me time to form an opinion of them - how accurately I do not know. Some of them "act" their whole lives but I pass on my observations of Mr. Kaye for what they are worth.

We set up our 16mm Arriflex camera and the Nagra ¼" audio tape recorder then lit the allocated hotel area accordingly. Mr Kaye strode in with a rather cynical air and sat down after the briefest of preliminary chats with the interviewer. It is customary in movie-making that when filming is about to begin the director calls *turnover*, the camera starts rolling and the audio tape recorder is switched on. When the recorder is up to speed the sound operator calls *speed*. The camera assistant holds an open clapper board containing the chalked shot-number in front of the camera then claps it to make a distinctive sound. This enables the picture and sound to be synchronised after processing to make editing possible. The director calls *action* and the scene proceeds.

On this particular day I was rather nervous about filming Danny Kaye, one of the first stars I had met as the producer of BBC2's new weekly programme *Film Night,* so I wanted to follow the correct procedures. All was ready, so I called out rather firmly *turnover*. At this point the star scathingly imitated me, indicating his disdain for my utterance. It was an unnecessary gesture and quite rude, even though I now understand how irksome such formalities can be with a tiny TV film unit when a movie star is accustomed to the workings of a 35mm film crew on a huge Hollywood sound stage.

The interview covered all aspects of his career as well as his untiring work for UNICEF, the children's charity. He was articulate and fairly succinct but there were no jokes. Afterwards he was more amenable. I knew he was a qualified pilot so I was impressed when he told me about the new Boeing 747s which were about to be launched in Europe. I remember him trying to give a semblance of how big the plane was. He did this by saying it had 16 toilets on board. Subsequently I have travelled the world on these aircraft but have never counted the WCs. For all I know he could be right.

I did not see Danny Kaye again until September 1980 when I was visiting Deauville in Normandy, the only French Film Festival devoted solely to American cinema. Much of the Deauville Film Festival took place beside the town's casino. Retrospective screenings of movies by old Hollywood stars was a feature of the Festival and the stars themselves usually made a personal appearance.

On my arrival, I did not know who this year's featured vintage star would be. I was there to film an interview with Clint Eastwood about his latest film *Bronco Billy*. My companion on this trip was the artist, Myles Antony, and he wanted to see the famous ornate but tiny opera house nearby. On our return to the screening area, I saw a Festival official leading a frail old man along the corridor. He was staring straight ahead and looked gaga. It was Danny Kaye. He was in his early 70s and looked 90. It was heartbreaking to see him like this. Myles and I went into the cinema.

An announcement was made and on stage came Danny Kaye. The applause was deafening. Danny Kaye came to life. He looked 50, his eyes clear and sharp. He made no speech - he simply pretended to be an orchestral conductor (another of his talents) and used his hands to orchestrate the applause. It was magical yet funny. I became a fan at last.

Four   Twelfth Night

I was not a good student at the University of Queensland. I was overwhelmed by the dedicated band of older, returned servicemen from World War II who were taking the opportunity of a lifetime by receiving a grant to study for a much-prized degree. They were streets ahead of me in wisdom, experience and dedication so I revelled instead in extra-curricular activities, particularly the University Dramatic and Choral Societies - all very time consuming, leaving little time for revision. The only subject I really enjoyed was History of Music. All I wanted to do was work in radio but banking was what my parents thought I should do. After their experiences during the 1930s Depression they wanted to make sure I had a *proper job*. So for a short time I became a bank teller.

I was happier as a member of the amateur Twelfth Night Theatre Group. I was surprised when I was selected to perform as 3rd servant to the Duke of Cornwall in *King Lear*. No doubt my limited experience with the University of Queensland Dramatic Society had paid off. I was never a good actor but my youth and appearance enabled me eventually to play the occasional leading role. I now realise the truth of G.K. Chesterton's maxim *if a thing's worth doing, it's worth doing badly.* Those amateur productions of the said *Lear, Twelfth Night* and *The Tempest,* in which I participated, were dire in retrospect, but during the many weeks of rehearsal I learned to enjoy and appreciate Shakespeare's verse far more than I had ever done at school or university.

While we were cavorting on the amateur stage, the professional theatre was enjoying a post-war boom. Thanks to British Arts Council sponsorship, I saw in Brisbane The Old Vic Company's production of the Restoration comedy *The School for Scandal* starring Laurence Olivier and Vivien Leigh. I had loved their movie performances but I had never seen stage acting like this.

I was mesmerised by Vivien Leigh's coquettish beauty and radiant, flawless complexion as she made her first entrance as Lady Teazle in a flowing black velvet dress. I was even more thrilled when I accompanied a local socialite to Brisbane's Debutante Ball, now such an anachronism but then a most desirable event. The debutantes were to be presented to - wait for it - the Oliviers.

We stood in line as they made their regal entrance and my heart sank as Miss Leigh walked about 2 feet away from me. That 'flawless complexion' was created by lots of makeup, swamped with powder. It was a lesson well learned. Consequently when I saw Britain's Royal Shakespeare Company perform *Much Ado About Nothing* in the same theatre, I had no desire to see what Anthony Quayle and Diana Wynyard, who played Beatrice and Benedick, looked like off-stage.

A few years later I had the opportunity of meeting the revered British actress Dame Sybil Thorndike and her husband Sir Lewis Casson at a reception in Brisbane preceding their poetry reading recital. They were both in their seventies and I had no preconceptions about them. She was born to act and, no doubt, to upstage everyone around her including her long suffering, somewhat irascible husband, but I loved every minute of her performance as Dame Sybil and enjoyed them both even more on stage. To hear poetry expertly interpreted by two superbly modulated voices with appropriate flashes of understated English humour was a revelation to a young, star-struck Australian in his early twenties.

My most successful role was the lead in Christopher Fry's *The Boy With A Cart*, a British playwright who is unpopular these days. His writing is now deemed pretentious. All I know is that he told a simple story using appealing and appropriate language which was so popular in Brisbane in the early 1950s that we had to repeat the production the following year in a larger theatre.

My role was originally played on the London stage by Richard Burton. He had also originated the part I had also played in Fry's best-known play *The Lady's Not For Burning*. Would this mean I could be a famous as he was? That was my ambition. Then I listened to his voice on radio in Dylan Thomas' *Under Milk Wood*. It had a resonance and clarity I could never emulate.

You can imagine what a thrill it was for me to listen to his voice in person when I filmed an interview with him in 1978 at London's Dorchester Hotel. He was promoting *The Wild Geese,* an adventure film about four British mercenaries in central Africa. As soon as we arrived, Burton proudly confessed to interviewer and crew alike that he was now 'on the wagon'. His gently pock-marked complexion added to his somewhat ravaged appearance - he certainly looked his 53 years despite his innate handsomeness. He enjoyed being one of the boys, swearing like a trouper while the lighting was being adjusted in the hotel suite assigned for the purpose - he was too professional to do so during the filming although I felt he was dying to, a Celtic anarchist through and through. Why is it so disconcerting to hear four letter words spoken so mellifluously?

Richard Burton had great charm and was more articulate than most actors I had met. He also spoke affectionately about his ex-wife, Elizabeth Taylor, which to me is always an endearing trait. It was a most pleasant afternoon, until the next scheduled interview with the former movie heartthrob, Stewart Granger, who was also in *The Wild Geese*.

Compared to Burton he was an unpleasant man with a big chip on his shoulder, trying to make nasty jokes at the expense of others. We did not transmit one frame of this second interview. The day after the Burton interview was televised, colleagues at BBC TV Centre told me *how well he had come across on TV*. This was inevitably followed by, *what was he really like?* How can one answer that? I knew Richard Burton for an afternoon, that's all. I had only seen him in person once before in my life, in Gstaad, Switzerland in 1975 when he had been reunited with his ex-wife, the beautiful but turbaned and dumpy Elizabeth Taylor.

They were attending a dinner given by Sir Lew Grade for the world's press to celebrate the success of his production *The Return of the Pink Panther*. Although neither he nor Taylor had any connection with the film, they were invited because they had a villa in Gstaad and were in town at the time. That evening at the next table to mine I saw Richard Burton behaving as the star he was. That afternoon in London he was a good bloke doing his job. Would the *real* Richard Burton please stand up? What I was unable to tell him was that his sonorous, lilting voice inspired me 25 years earlier and provided me with the determination to work in radio - as an announcer.

I applied in secret while I still held my *proper job* to become a General Cadet at the Australian Broadcasting Commission's Queensland Branch. I would be trained in all aspects of broadcasting, but *not* as an announcer. I never became what I wanted to be. I would not have been good at it either. It was simply the passion to work in radio which set me on a path I knew not where.

Five   Radio Times

On my first day at the Australian Broadcasting Commission's air conditioned offices in Brisbane in January 1951, just days after my 21st birthday, I was overawed to meet Ray Barrett. He was the contract actor who appeared in all their drama productions. I spoke to him in my deepest voice which I had hoped to adopt permanently so that I may be considered as a radio announcer at a later date. Like many actors he liked his booze but it never affected his performances - it may have even enhanced them.

As well as being an instinctive actor, he also was musical with a more than passable baritone. A few years later we made some Road Safety commercials together - he sang ridiculous lyrics while I accompanied him uneasily on the piano. We lost contact when he moved to Sydney to bigger and better things but we met up again in 1968 at BBC TV Centre in London. He was just as pleasant and easy-going as ever, although by then he was one of the stars of the hit BBC TV drama series *The Troubleshooters* and the voice of John Tracy in the even more popular *Thunderbirds* puppet series.

Like most Australian actors in the 1950s he wanted to try his luck in the UK. By 1957 he was playing Dr. Nolan in ITV's first twice-weekly serial *Emergency Ward 10*. In 1965 he played Peter Thornton in a BBC series *Mogul* about the Mogul oil company which changed its title the following year to *The Troubleshooters*. When the Australian government set up the Australian Film Commission in the early 1970s and the feature film industry flourished there, Ray returned to Oz and played mostly character roles in movies and TV mini-series. I shall always treasure our perfunctory friendship.

As an ABC trainee I became a jack-of-all-trades. I was asked to record the occasional radio interview using a strange (pre-audio tape) wire recorder. The first interview I ever did was with the retiring U.S. Consul to Brisbane. I was given a stopwatch as the interview had to last 4 minutes and there were no editing facilities. I doubt if I was very welcoming to my guest when he arrived at the studio. I was trying desperately to conceal the fact that this was my initiation. I had written down all my questions in their correct order and, being terribly nervous, asked them one after the other as written. When I asked question four, the Consul's reply began, *well, as I've just said*, etc. ...I was mortified but I learned a valuable lesson about radio interviewing. The hardest thing to do is to listen to what is being said when there are so many distractions. To help the interviewee, who is often nervous, one should give encouragement and acknowledgement through one's eyes. I did not look even once at the American consul during that discouraging interview. Strange to say, it was broadcast the next day.

The first Hollywood star I interviewed was Diana Barrymore, daughter of the great John, he with the perfect profile. I was 22 and she was a star in my eyes, my closest link so far to magical Hollywood. She was in Brisbane on tour in a play, the title of which totally escapes me. I took my wire recorder with me to the then famous Lennon's Hotel and eventually met the great John Barrymore's actress daughter. She had a scar on her left cheek as if someone had once slashed her with a beer bottle which, I discovered later, might have been the case. Her eyes had a glassy look about them, she barely wore any makeup and I was sadly disappointed. Where was the glamour I craved? She was only 31. I had only seen her in one film, the second half of a double bill, which starred Loretta Young. It was *Ladies Courageous* and Diana was one of a group in the U.S. Women's Air Force during World War II.

The interview was wholly unmemorable and even starry-eyed me sensed she had drunk one too many the night before. A few years later her biography *Too Much Too Soon* was published. The 1958 film version starring Errol Flynn as her father, John Barrymore, with Dorothy Malone as his wayward daughter, was more successful than poor Diana's life had ever been. She died before her 40th birthday.

As an interviewer I improved gradually with my technique but never felt it was my natural calling. However, years later in London that experience was to stand me in good stead as a means of earning a living.

When I was working in the ABC Music Department, it was run by the talented concert pianist, Allen McCristal. He was one of the worst and laziest managers I ever encountered. I liked him a lot. His secretary, Pam Dearden, did all the donkey work as well as providing the odd bit of shorthand and typing for various celebrities. Each year, thanks to the ABC, Australia had a steady stream of overseas musicians to give concerts with the local ABC-run symphony orchestras, as well as celebrity solo recitals in five Australian states. When the noted American violinist, Isaac Stern, came to Brisbane as part of his tour, he dictated Pam five letters then counted out five sheets of *Isaac Stern* headed note-paper. He said he would return a few hours later to sign them. That day Isaac Stern made Pam a nervous wreck. No error was expected or possible.

In 1983 I was going down in the crowded elevator at London's National Theatre (the Royal prefix came later) after a performance of the ill-fated Marvin Hamlisch musical *Jean,* about the tragic Hollywood star Jean Seberg. I realised that the small rotund grey-haired figure beside me was Maestro Stern himself. I did not tell him how mean he was about his personalised stationery but I wanted to. Despite our silence he knew that I knew who he was. It is something all celebrities notice but pretend they don't.

After I moved from Brisbane to Sydney in 1957, I saw the Russian composer, Igor Stravinsky, conduct one of his own compositions with the Sydney Symphony Orchestra. I saw the Spanish soprano, Victoria de los Angeles sing exquisitely. She was not very tall with a stout chest and black, shining hair swept into a bun. She exuded charm and confidence and the audiences loved her. I laughed uproariously at the operatic antics of the comedienne Anna Russell and the cheeky satirical songs written and sung at the piano by the American wit Tom Lehrer.

I saw Australia's best known diva Joan Sutherland in *La Traviata* and *Lucia di Lammermoor* when she introduced audiences in 1965 to a young tenor almost at the start of his operatic career, Luciano Pavarotti. I attended many Gilbert & Sullivan operettas by Britain's D'Oyly Carte Opera Co. where I first heard a contralto sound like a car changing gear when she moved from her chest to her head register, a condition to which many contraltos are prone.

I saw concerts given by Frank Sinatra, Judy Garland and jazz pianist Dave Brubeck at Sydney Stadium where their stage was a boxing ring. Judy walked past me at the end of her performance to ecstatic applause. I called out to her *good on you, Judy,* a comment which embarrasses me to this day. I watched Britain's Ballet Rambert perform several times; I saw John Gielgud in his one-man show *The Seven Ages of Man*; Maurice Chevalier (I even met him at his Press Conference) as the legendary French boulevardier; and Jack

Benny, America's funniest comedian who played the violin better than he let on. I was entranced by Katharine Hepburn as Portia to Robert Helpmann's Shylock in *The Merchant of Venice*. I hope this proves the absurdity of that rather funny joke.

What's the difference between Australia and yoghurt?

Yoghurt has a culture.

In March 1957, a few months after television had started in Australia, I was given a production job with ABC Children's Department in Sydney where I could continue using my radio skills whilst gaining experience in the new medium. For a time I played Tabby Cat in the radio serial *The Muddleheaded Wombat* whilst presenting a weekly stamp programme on TV. By 1960 I had gone freelance and four years later I received an offer which became the watershed of my life - a free inaugural Air India flight to London.

In the few days I was in London I saw on the West End stage the Welsh actress Rachel Roberts in the new Lionel Bart musical *Maggie May* at the Adelphi Theatre. I was impressed by the acting, the staging and the wonderful sound of the pit orchestra, more streamlined than Australian productions. I saw a stage version of Iris Murdoch's novel *A Severed Head* but jet lag got the better of me and I slept fitfully through the second half. I managed to get a ticket to the Royal Opera House to see Luchino Visconti's wonderful production of Verdi's *Il Trovatore* with, if memory serves me right, the young Welsh soprano Gwyneth Jones making her Covent Garden debut in a leading role.

I also visited my two maiden great-aunts on a day trip to Blackpool. They took me for a walk along the Promenade. I can still feel the chill November wind off the Irish Sea blowing on my sun-tanned Australian face and I shall never forget my first glimpse of what they called a beach. It was pathetic by Aussie standards - no soft white sand, no blue water with exciting waves to surf on, just a grey foreshore, muddy water and a bleak sky.

By now I was married with two young children so when I returned to a loving family in a comfortable Sydney suburban house with all mod cons, the azure blue sky above and tall eucalyptus trees all around, I was so happy. This was where I really wanted to live. I had this satisfied feeling for precisely three weeks!

I could not wait to see more of the world and visit again that exciting metropolis London. This coincided with my disillusionment with Australian TV. The egalitarian society did not help. In those days nobody seemed to care whether we made a good TV programme or not.

Nothing was going to stop me from returning to 'swinging London'. When I was a teenager, my grandmother had unwittingly given me my philosophy of life. We were enjoying a lovely picnic on a sandy beach in sunny Sydney. She turned and said *this and better will do me.* I was about to look for something better.

Six   Bush House & the BBC

My saviour in London was the Australian-born broadcaster Malcolm Billings, who left Sydney in 1963 and quickly established himself in radio on the BBC especially at their World Service headquarters in Bush House, a magnificent building in The Aldwych at the end of Kingsway.

He and his wife and young son lived in a nice flat in the leafy suburb of Highgate, North London. When I contacted him from Sydney about my impending visit to London, he offered me temporary accommodation at his apartment. And so it came to pass that I arrived in London one Sunday in late May 1966 with £100 to tide me over until I found work. I had brought with me various letters of introduction and thought this would suffice.

I followed up all but one of my contacts and the very person I bypassed was the very person who gave me my first TV opportunity two years later. I could have saved myself much time and energy if I had contacted him straight away but life is not like that.

On that first Sunday night in London, Malcolm suggested that I go with him the next morning to Bush House. He would introduce me to producers for freelance radio interview work. I protested that it was not fair if I were to compete with him. He simply replied, *there's enough work for the two of us.* That is what I call a true friend and that is how I became a full-time radio reporter for 8 months and a part-time one for another year and a bit. It was not my forte, I knew that, but I would give it a try. That first morning I was commissioned to make a 15 minute programme for the *Postmark UK* series about a place called Enfield. I did not even know where it was - it certainly held no place on the Monopoly Board, my prime source of knowledge of London property and landmarks.

Later in the week I put my head around the door of one office in Bush House and the producer, who needed someone to cover the Chelsea Flower Show that day, sent me there with my tape recorder, even though I barely knew the names of any English flowers apart from roses and asters. And so the work grew. Malcolm also introduced me to a programme producer who immediately engaged me to provide a weekly pop star interview slot. Of course I accepted even though I barely knew one British pop star from another, except for Cliff Richard. I bought *New Musical Express* each week and soon became au fait with the pop scene of 'Swinging London'.

I am amazed that I got to meet and interview 1960s stars like Cilla Black who behaved rather grandly behind-the scenes, despite her cosy image; The Small Faces, a cute quartet whose leader, Steve Marriott, was burnt to death in a fire at his modest home 30 years later; singing duo Peter and Gordon, the former being actress Jane Asher's brother who eventually settled in Los Angeles and became a top record producer; Procul Harum who had just released their first song *A Whiter Shade of Pale* which later became a classic; a charming pop singer called Mark Wynter during a Summer Season on one of Blackpool's famous piers; and The Bachelors, a fairly boring (to talk to) trio of young Irishmen who sang amiably in harmony. Once I went by train to

Bournemouth to interview the popular Australian group The Seekers who were appearing there in a summer show. Sitting opposite me in the carriage were a father and son, both army types with posh accents.

Father: *Which car are you taking to the Royal Fusiliers Ball?*

Son: *The Jaguar*

Father: *Who are you taking?*

Son: *Lavinia.*

They got off at Basingstoke where cars are more important than people. The Seekers weren't posh and gave me a friendly down-to-earth interview, having just released one of their best-known hits *The Carnival Is Over.*

.I had plenty of work. I did not know it at the time but Malcolm was also used regularly at Broadcasting House by the Home Service (later BBC Radio 4) as an interviewer on presenter Jack De Manio's popular *Today* programme, which had a huge listening audience but paid the same six guineas per interview as the less prestigious World Service. However there was one advantage. The *Today* programme often repeated interviews the same day and sometimes yet again on their weekend compilation. Every time this happened the interviewer received a repeat fee, a proportion of the original.

This was the state of affairs when Malcolm and his then wife left for the Mediterranean island of Elba for a 5 week vacation. I stayed and looked after their London place, monitored their phone calls and watered their indoor plants, a recent interior design ploy. The British musical duo Flanders and Swann, had released a song on LP with the lyrics:

We're terribly 'House & Garden'
now that we've been given the chance

The garden's full of furniture and the house is full of plants.

The day after Malcolm left, I answered the phone.

Is Malcolm Billings there?

No, he is on holiday for 5 weeks.

Oh dear, it's the BBC Today programme here. We wanted him for an interview.

Would I do? I enquired as positively as I could under the circumstances.

Well, we are in a bit of a fix. Can you be here at Broadcasting House in 45 minutes?

Certainly, I replied confidently, having little idea whether or not I could make it.

See you in 45 minutes. The BBC producer put down the phone.

In a panic I put on my jacket, fled down from Highgate to Kentish Town underground station on the Northern Line, changed to the Central Line at Tottenham Court Rd, got off at Oxford Circus and raced into Broadcasting House just in time. Here was my big chance and I had only been in England ten days.

The interview in the plush studio had to last 2 ½ minutes - they did not want to have to edit it - and it was about the casting of a pig in a Bertie Wooster TV series about to be filmed for BBC1. I had never read P.G. Wodehouse, the creator of *Jeeves and Wooster* - their lives had seemed so irrelevant and outmoded to me in Australia and now I wished I had. My task was to interview the charming and witty TV Light Entertainment producer, Michael Mills. He was a real 'pro'. After an initial question or two, he told one funny story after another about how he went about finding a suitable animal to play the Marchioness of Blandford, the most unlikely name for a sow.

I was a terrible interviewer that day, worse than usual by trying to ensure that the piece ran to time, and I was in unfamiliar surroundings. The producer neither praised nor thanked me - just asked for the address to which the six guinea cheque should be sent. I knew this would be the first and last time I would enter the hallowed portals of the world famous BBC Broadcasting House. I was devastated.

The next morning I set the alarm for 7am to listen to *Today* on the off chance that my appalling interview would be scheduled. Sure enough it was broadcast. I was astonished when it was repeated later that morning, flabbergasted when it was included in the weekend compilation. Michael Mills was such a good interviewee that my contribution was immaterial. He had made my day. Later when I was working at BBC TV Centre I saw Michael Mills often as he dashed from one production to another. Naturally he did not recognise me. I never mustered up the courage to thank him for talking so eloquently and amusingly about a pig.

Just eleven days after my arrival in London, the phone rang. I was hoping there would be an offer of another interview at Bush House but there wasn't. It was the BBC *Today* programme. They wanted me to interview the Japanese Ambassador to London about the impending tour of Japan by the Beatles. *This would be easier than yesterday*, I thought, *a chance to redeem myself.* Wrong. No matter how well a Japanese ambassador speaks English, he will still get his 'r's and 'l's confused. I had blown my second chance on *Today*. How could I do a decent interview when I could barely understand the answers? I went home dejected. Next morning I tuned in. It was the second item broadcast and, yet again, it was repeated twice.

The next day the *Today* programme rang me once more. I knew I was on safer ground because this time I would be interviewing a Scotsman. A radio link with the Faroe Islands had been arranged by my producer. Scotland was challenging Denmark's sovereignty of the islands in a rather half-hearted way and the BBC wanted reaction from a resident. The producer had all the background information to the story. He briefed me well and together we compiled the appropriate questions to ask the Scotsman. In the studio the radio link was established, the tape recording machine was switched on and the interview commenced. The line was crackling so that is possibly why I did not understand one word the Scotsman said in the broadest of dialects. The Japanese Ambassador had been easy compared to this.

The five weeks passed and hardly a day went by without *Today* using me for an interview. It was, after all, the start of the *silly season*, a phrase unknown to me in the Antipodes, but one to which I adapted quickly. In those days annual leave was taken in June, July or August, no-one venturing much further than Spain or Italy, with most holidaymakers spending their vacations in Britain. I had arrived in England at the right time. Without *the silly season* my career might not have taken off. Malcolm and his wife returned refreshed from Elba and I was glad to have their company in the flat again. I was missing my family in Australia and was not used to living alone for weeks at a time. After talking about their holiday over supper, we sat down to watch TV. The phone rang, Malcolm answered.

Hello, Malcolm Billings.

It's BBC Today programme here. Could I speak to Barry Brown please?

The fight was on. No longer were we colleagues but competitors. I moved into a cheap bedsit in Belsize Park so Malcolm and I saw only each other at either Bush or Broadcasting House. It was all quite jovial but there was a touch of rivalry there.

I was given assignments outside the studio. Once I went by train to Farnborough in Hampshire to interview the new women's world gliding champion. I asked her what was the highest she had ever gone in her glider. It was 35,000 feet. *Accidentally*, she hastened to add. It turned me off gliding for life.

Another interviewee, the travel writer and author Elspeth Huxley, talked with me about my homeland. She said what she found interesting was that Australia was a foreign country where English was spoken.

In due course, I had saved enough to buy a car and so I was sent far and wide to interview a variety of people. Once I drove to Letchworth in Hertfordshire at 2am to cover a World Knitting Marathon. Another time I travelled to Essex to record a remarkable event in a suburban house - whenever the owner took out his false teeth, his dog, no matter where it was, would start whining. To prove it I took my tape recorder into the back garden with the dog, while the owner remained in the kitchen towards the front of the house. Sure enough within a few seconds the dog whined. I checked and the owner had his teeth in his hand! I also interviewed the soprano Heather Harper, when she sang Act I of an opera at Covent Garden, changed quickly as she dashed to the Festival Hall to replace an ill singer in an oratorio performance, then raced back to perform in Act III at the Royal Opera House. I admired such professionalism.

I was surprised how much work I was given by the *Today* producers. I was reliable. I would record each interview myself, edit it down to 2 ½ minutes on my own machine, write an introduction for Jack De Manio to read, state the 'start' and 'end' words of the interview, and on the same sheet of paper give an accurate duration of the piece and my name and address for payment, all simple and efficient. To my mind, some of those *Today* radio producers were a lazy lot - so much so that two of them were later given high profile managerial jobs with commercial TV stations and earned a fortune.

The strangest experience was when I had to perform some political subterfuge. The on-duty *Today* producer wanted reaction to some political event which now escapes me, from a member of the House of Commons and from the House of Lords but neither was to know I was interviewing the other. The MP chosen was the Liberal, David Steel, the peer chosen was Labour's Lord Dilhorne. It was late at night when I arrived with my tape recorder.

In those days security was farcically lax. I could easily have equalled and maybe surpassed Guy Fawkes' performance centuries earlier. I told the policeman on duty I was from the BBC and he showed me how to reach David Steel's office. My bag and recorder were not checked. When I completed the interview, Mr Steel directed me out of the building. I then walked a few yards and asked another policeman on duty at the Palace of Westminster how to get to Lord Dilhorne's office. He gave me vague directions and I got lost. It was dark and rather menacing and I found myself in a beautiful but unlit library. I could have stolen a precious tome or two and no one would have been any the wiser. After completing the second interview I left the building. *Good night, sir,* said the policeman and that was it. For all he knew, a few minutes later a bomb or two could have wrecked both Houses of Parliament.

Innocence enabled me to achieve almost anything. Working as a freelance, mostly at Bush House, I decided to be more enterprising and, rather than wait for commissions, would do some 'on spec' interviews to rake in a few extra six guinea fees. I contacted the Postmaster General's PR man and arranged an interview with the then Postmaster-General, Anthony Wedgwood-Benn, later to be known as Tony Benn MP.

On the appointed day at the appointed time, I was shown into the Postmaster Generals' sumptuous office and during the interview he revealed many aspects of his new job, including an increased number of stamp issues. His PR man hovered during the recording. As I was leaving he seemed most agitated. *The Postmaster-General has told you things that haven't been announced yet,* he muttered as I left their splendid City headquarters. When I offered the interview to a programme editor at Bush House, he was delighted but aghast.

How did you manage to get it?

I replied honestly, *I rang up his office and arranged it.*

He then explained BBC protocol in which permission had to be granted by an executive with a highfalutin' title before any politician could be interviewed. It was one way of maintaining a balance between 'on air' time given to political parties. The producer must have obtained a belated clearance. All I know is that the interview was broadcast and I received my cheque.

I knew from experience that before one goes out on the road to record a radio interview, one should always check the reel-to-reel tape machine to ensure that there is a take-up spool already in place. From experience one also learns to take a spare reel of blank tape in case the proposed short interview lasts longer than 15 minutes because, at a speed of 19cms per second, that is when the tape runs out. I had an appointment with the Duke of Bedford at his glorious estate Woburn Abbey in Buckinghamshire, over an hour's drive (in those days) from London. I was late in leaving Bush House owing to a protracted phone call, so I grabbed my tape recorder in its hold-all without checking its contents, raced to where my car was parked and set off.

As a gawky tourist I had visited this stately home but the private apartments were equally impressive. The Duke was affable, charming and wonderfully urbane. He told me the Rembrandt hanging on the wall behind him was bought by an ancestor for £16. Like all good aristocrats, he had an appreciation of the absurd. I could tell this was going to be a good interview. I saw a spare reel of tape in my bag which was handy because I wanted this to be a long interview. I took out my tape recorder, opened the lid and there was no take-up spool. So while the Duke chatted away in the usual pre-performance preamble, I quietly put a pencil through the centre of the spare spool and wound off one whole spare reel of unused tape in order to give me the much-needed take-up spool. It would now have to be a short interview contained on one reel. I noticed that the waste paper bin into which the tape had coiled was of embossed Italian leather. The Duke made no comment, bless him. With take-up spool in place, the interview proceeded beautifully and ended just before the tape ran out, more good luck than good management.

I must add what might be an apocryphal story about the film actor James Mason, a personal friend of the Duke and Duchess of Bedford. After making the film *Age of Consent* in Australia he had married Clarissa Kaye, a local actress who was also in the film. Her parents were visiting their daughter and son-in-law in England when James and his wife were invited to a weekend house party at Woburn Abbey. He explained that he had relatives staying with him so they went too. On the first afternoon the butler was serving tea comprising cucumber sandwiches, scones with strawberry jam and cream and a sponge cake. He looked at Mrs Kaye and said *China or Indian, madam*. Her simple response was, *we're Australian.*

Fairly early on in my Bush House sojourn, I was put in charge of a 15-minute weekly programme for Australians in Australia. Its purpose was to reflect and promote life in the UK. I researched all the stories, pre-recorded the interviews, then wrote and narrated the programme. There was rarely any hierarchical interference, it was wonderful. Each edition had to run 13 minutes 30 seconds exactly. It was then transferred from audio tape to disc and despatched by air to Australia. It was not broadcast on BBC World Service only in Australia itself.

When I emerged from the studio after the recording of the first edition, I was told my editing time would be early the next morning. *What for?* I asked.

To edit the programme to its correct duration was the reply. *The programme has to run 13 minutes 30 seconds exactly.*

I know and that's how long it runs - exactly!

My bosses were amazed. I was trained the Antipodean way. It was the producer's job to *make* a programme run to time. And that is what I did, right to the final second. I soon adjusted to the British way. It was less stressful, more rewarding and the finished product was superior. I liked the way people worked in the UK. Everything was more considered, more thought-provoking and of a higher standard. I remembered yet again my grandmother's philosophy of life, *this and better will do me.*

I fitted in comfortably to the BBC way of doing things. Having freelanced in Australia and the UK for nearly seven years, I was adamant that I would remain self-employed and never work for a large organisation again. That determination did not last long. Out of the blue I was offered a one year BBC staff contract. I accepted and began unwittingly a career with the BBC which lasted 28 years.

Seven   The Road to Television

My BBC contract with the World Service was to produce 3 editions a week of a new 45 minute magazine programme for expatriates overseas called *Outlook*. The producer I was replacing had been seconded to Nigerian TV for a year. I realised I had become an experienced exponent of magazine programmes. I enjoyed the mix of spoken word with relevant music and a variety of material at my disposal. It was my job to make it as interesting and stimulating as possible.

What I commissioned and how I incorporated that into *Outlook* was a daily challenge and I loved every minute of it. There were three presenters, one of whom, John Tidmarsh, was still introducing the programme more than thirty years later. The top items in each programme concentrated on current affairs, with lighter stories further down the list. It was a good mix and it was really popular with expatriates all round the globe. What their servants thought of it is another matter. Even in the late 1960s such programmes were rather colonial in their attitude and tone.

Although I had 9 years of TV experience in Australia behind me, I was working in radio in London, because no matter whom I approached in British TV, I was treated patronisingly.

Australia was once referred to in my presence as *one of the colonies* - and he wasn't joking. It soon became apparent that despite the occasional hiccup, I was accepted for who I was. I did not want or need to return to Australia so the family followed by ship, as planned. After such a long separation, it was not a happy reunion and eventually we divorced.

My boss at BBC World Service was Douglas Muggeridge a cousin once or twice removed from the celebrated pundit Malcolm. He could tell I was an experienced producer and he knew I wanted to get into TV production so he arranged for me to see a BBC Personnel Officer, a balding man with a grey face and a grey suit. In his unappealing office I gave him 'the big sell'. He was not used to such bravado. After a while he said, *are you sure you want to produce television and not perform on it, as you are giving me a good performance at the moment?* I was mortified. I was being 'myself'. Was there anything wrong with giving some kind of *performance* if you really wanted a job? Perhaps he wanted to meet a shrinking violet so that he could tell me that I was unsuitable for TV. It is much easier to say 'no'. The buck stops there.

I came away somewhat crestfallen from that interview. The second BBC TV channel, BBC 2, had been on the air for nearly 4 years and seemed to be taking on more staff month after month, but not me. What's more, there was a nightly programme called *Late Night Line-Up* which was being transmitted in colour as an experiment. I tried to catch a glimpse colour TV whenever I could - mainly in shop windows.

To my surprise, as a result of that abortive interview with the man from Personnel, I was invited to apply for an Assistant Producer job on *Late Night Line-Up*. I was not selected but must have made a good impression. I was offered a short-term contract as a Production Assistant for the princely sum of £37 a week. This was 1968 and I was used to earning more in radio. I accepted only on condition that after three month's probation, if I proved satisfactory, I would be promoted to Producer on a higher salary.

The man who employed me was Rowan Ayers, the person I had neglected to contact two years earlier. Those two years of radio experience truly prepared me for what lay ahead in TV. I now knew my way around London and knew how to deal with people in *this foreign country where English was spoken*. I was beginning to understand the British psyche.

I arrived at White City just before 9.30am, as requested, on a sunny May morning to start my new job. There was no-one there. Eventually someone arrived and I was introduced to those on duty - *Late Night Line-Up* was a seven-day-a-week operation. Several others drifted in later when it suited them, it was all rather casual. As it was such a hot day, we all got into cars at lunch time and drove to a wonderful pub right on the Thames near Hammersmith Bridge, drank beer and ate ham sandwiches.

After two hours we drifted back to TV Centre. I was a little the worse for wear as I was unaccustomed to alcohol in the middle of the day. The programme was put together for that evening, the script vaguely written, which included a small contribution suggested and compiled by me and went to air 'live' around 11pm. At last I was working in BBC TV. I was looking forward to more of those lovely lunches by the river. It never happened again.

On the second day there was a quite different atmosphere in the office. The Editor's estranged wife had committed suicide. On the third day a colleague announced he was taking an early lunch and left the open-plan office. What I did not know was that he had put a pre-recorded message on a portable tape recorder, pressed the *PLAY* button, locked it in a nearby cupboard and departed the building. A few minutes later (he had timed it perfectly), I heard a knock on a cupboard door, then a muffled voice said *let me out, let me out,* followed by more frantic door rapping. I was aghast. I did not know what to do. I tried to open the cupboard. It was locked. And still the frantic noise continued. Then the penny dropped, it was a practical joke. *Late Night Line-Up* was like that.

The main thrust of the programme was a late night review of that day's television output, not exclusively from the BBC. After, say, *Play for Today* or the current affairs flagship programme *Panorama*, a hastily assembled group of critics would be paid a meagre ten guineas to arrive at TV Centre, watch the programme from B055, the basement hospitality suite (where sometimes they drank too much), catch the elevator up to the fourth floor for a dab of make-up, then into the tiny studio where they would brutally dissect the programme. You can imagine how popular it was with other BBC production departments. There were many attempts to censor, even close down, the nightly programme but it survived until December 1972.

The main presenters while I worked there were Tony Bilbow, a writer and journalist with glasses and a pudding basin haircut; Michael Dean, a good-looking New Zealander whom I had known in Australian radio; Sheridan Morley, the actor Robert's son with an equally booming voice; and Joan Bakewell who had recently been labelled *the thinking man's crumpet*. I admired their ability to chair 'live' discussions with sometimes belligerent guests or to interview a wide range of contributors on a variety of topics.

Originally the interviews were with TV performers, directors, producers, critics etc., but, as it was a daily programme, the scope increased to include film and pop stars when they were in town or classical and folk musicians. *Late Night Line-Up* had a store of standby material on videotape - as all good 'live' magazine TV programmes do - to be used when a discussion fell through, a guest failed to turn up or an 'on-air' item ended early. Sheridan Morley was able to arrange a studio interview with the visiting film actress Viveca Lindfors. Originally from Sweden, she started making Hollywood movies after World War II, few of them memorable. She was a vivacious woman but she was rather long-winded and although still photogenic in her early fifties, the interview entered the standby zone. Whenever an extra item was needed someone would offer the Viveca Lindfors interview. Then back it would go on to the standby shelf. It became a running joke. Long after I had left the *Line-Up* production team, I was home watching the programme late one evening when up on the TV screen came Viveca Lindfors. She had made it to air just before the programme's demise. The interview had been lying around for nearly 3 years. As she had made no movies during that time, the interview was still relevant.

While I was a Production Assistant I was given the chance to direct in the tiny TV studio where all editions of *Late Night Line-Up* and ancillary programmes emanated. It was for our sole use, a facility few TV producers experience. It did not have to be booked in advance and paid for. Other producers from other parts of the BBC had to compete for their studio time. We were very lucky but did not appreciate the luxury it afforded us. *Line-Up*, being the last programme of the evening, had no set duration - it ended when it ended - which was another luxury and one which was occasionally abused. Some editions went on far too long, it was sheer self indulgence.

Nevertheless they provided a healthy outlet for TV criticism which has never been paralleled. The programme's output expanded and music items were needed to supplement the spoken word. As I could read a score, I directed many musicians performing one or two pieces, which were pre-recorded for later use as individual items. On one occasion I had a huge blown-up black-and-white portrait of Mozart, suffused with soft green lighting, below which the composer's oboe quartet was performed by two men and two women in black evening dress, led by the oboist Janet Craxton. It looked rather good and certainly different (up until then the studio was always blue lit) and as the studio was so tiny, I was vision mixer as well as director. This required a new set of skills so I was rather nervous.

One time a producer watching from behind tapped me on the shoulder and said *trigger happy*. He was right. From then on I used fewer camera shots and angles. When the popular African folk singer Miriam Makeba came to the studio to perform, I used the shadow of a hastily erected pole from which hung a hangman's noose in order to illustrate her songs of oppression. *Very symbolic* I thought, but Miriam was a large lady, dressed in maroon with matching material swathed round her head in that African way and was charismatic enough to simply stand there and sing. She made no comment on my attempted set design. Thank you, Miriam.

No score was available when Tim Hardin, the American singer-songwriter, came with his fellow musicians into the studio. He had written that famous 1960s song *If I Were a Carpenter* and he was to record that and another song for later transmission. I was diligent and listened well in advance to his recordings, worked out a shot list (stating where the cameras would be placed and what type of shots would be required) and entered the studio with a modicum of self confidence. The rehearsal began. My pre-planned shots did not work for some reason. I made amendments and tried again. This time the run-through was worse. I became so tense that I did not realise that each time the group played a song, they performed it differently. By mid-afternoon nothing had been recorded and Tim needed a break.

I assumed he had gone to the tiny dressing-cum-make-up room beside Presentation 'B' - the name of the studio. Let me remind you *assumption is the mother of all cock-ups*. How was I to know that Tim Harden was a heroin addict? He had driven back to his hotel for another fix. In retrospect, I was surprised he returned but he did so with barely 20 minutes of recording time left. I got the cameramen to get whatever shots they could and I would 'wing' it, which is what I should have done in the first place. We only recorded one song. A few years later I was not surprised when I read that the troubled artist had died at an early age.

From those *Late Night Line-Up* musical forays emerged an offshoot programme called *The Old Grey Whistle Test* with my colleague Mike Appleton at the helm. It was a ground-breaking programme and featured all the top musicians of the day. It continued long after *Line-Up's* demise and Mike went on to produce the historic award-winning *Live Aid* concert in 1985.

Another directing assignment filled me with dread. The notorious Fanny Cradock, now past her prime, had been engaged to present a cookery series in the tiny studio, this time without her husband and sidekick Johnnie. She was a real pro and I liked her despite the occasional tantrum. She went her way and I went hers.

Her students did the preparation and handed her things during the recording but Fanny, groomed for a night at the opera, was always in charge, preparing a range of dishes no calorie-conscious restaurant would serve these days. How *Late Night Line-Up* became involved with Fanny Craddock I no longer remember but the producer of that series, Betty White, found another cook to take her place - Delia Smith. That was over 40 years ago. She became ever more popular on TV than Fanny.

The occasional interviews with film stars and directors, developed into another BBC2 offshoot, *Film Night* presented by Tony Bilbow and Philip Jenkinson. It ran for 8 years. I was its only producer.

Eight   Film Night

My three months as a Production Assistant on *Late Night Line-Up* were up. True to his word the editor Rowan Ayers called a staff meeting in August 1968 and announced that I would produce the Saturday night film programme, which, from September would have a regular late night Friday slot. What did I know about movies? I knew as much as anyone else in *Late Night Line-Up* apart from a freelance contract presenter Philip Jenkinson, a vintage movie buff, from whose collection clips would be used in the programme each week.

His slot on Saturday night had proven very popular and he received many requests to show favourite scenes from old movies. The Saturday night show, in my opinion, had been clobbered together by a colleague who had other production responsibilities, and an unimaginative and lazy researcher. Everything seemed to be done at the last minute.

In order to show clips, one had to request them from film distribution companies. In those days the clips were chosen by them and delivered on either 35mm (the standard cinema gauge) or 16mm (the standard TV gauge) film. The same clips would appear on the BBC as well as commercial TV's weekly show *Cinema*. These clips would be made up into one big roll and played into the programme on cue from the presenter. That's all it was. To me it was horribly amateurish.

What's more, because of its shift system, staff on *Late Night Line-Up* were notoriously unreliable at returning borrowed material, be it photographs, books, LP records or film clips. This was going to change.

So that my programme would be not be confused with *Line-Up's* reputation within the industry, I called it *Film Night*. Its success was dependent upon people lending me things. If I were reliable and collected material when I said I would and returned it on time, film companies and publicists would lend me anything. I needed their support to make a visually interesting programme about the current movie scene. I insisted on reliability from my small team and in due course it paid off.

However, I did not realise until it was too late that the Producer's Assistant allocated to me had previously only worked in radio and had been given this temporary job after a nervous breakdown. As I was still the new recruit, I got the short straw. Her incompetence and nervous disposition contributed to a memorable first edition of *Film Night*.

As well as being producer, I was the director and also vision mixer. I had never participated so acutely in a 'live' programme from this studio before. We rehearsed as best we could with Tony Bilbow and Philip Jenkinson. They were no problem. Their scripts were on autocue - the film clips simply had to be played into the programme at the right moment. A 16mm film clip had to be played in from a telecine machine two floors below the studio. Those machines needed 8 seconds to build up the correct speed. So 8 seconds before a film clip was required, on a designated word in the script, my assistant had to call down a microphone linked to the telecine area, these two simple words - *run telecine*. She was so terrified at rehearsal that she said nothing - she was dumbstruck. This did not augur well.

The rehearsal was a shambles and at the end of it she started sobbing and announced *I can't do it, I can't do it.* I tried to reassure her during the technical checks that are made before a 'live' transmission, to no avail. I had to add a fourth string to my bow and be a Producer's Assistant. I did as best I could under the circumstances but clips were shown late, leaving both presenters with *egg on their faces.* I 'cut' from several shots when I should have 'mixed' and I had no idea how long the programme was running. That was the least of my worries.

All I now remember about the programme was that it featured a section on Vivien Leigh who had died the previous year. I, too, nearly died after that programme. I do not remember being admonished the following Monday morning by my editor - perhaps he had gone to bed early and not seen it. All I insisted on was that I be given a competent assistant. The girl with the nervous breakdown returned to BBC radio.

I had a lot to learn. One early lesson concerned Cinemascope, a widescreen format that had been popular since *The Robe* started the trend in 1953. Many 1960s movies were made that way including *Boom!* starring Elizabeth Taylor and Richard Burton. I chose a clip from this film to open one edition of *Film Night* which, as I've explained, was transmitted 'live'.

In TV in those days a telecine operator would pan and scan the widescreen picture manually so that it fitted the smaller 4x3 ratio of a TV screen. At rehearsal I was devastated. I had chosen a scene between Taylor and Burton on the balcony of a villa overlooking the sea from the lovely Italian island of Ischia. The scene started. You could hear Burton talking but all you could see was the view from the balcony. He was on the far left of the screen out of view. The operator panned left until he reached Burton, which was the precise moment he stopped talking and Liz Taylor spoke. The operator panned slowly to the right of the screen, reaching her just as she finished her speech. And so it went on throughout the entire clip. It was marginally better during the actual telecast (I had no replacement clip at this late stage) but I and, no doubt the audience, felt seasick as the picture veered constantly from left to right and back again.

I had a researcher working temporarily with me who had an arrogant telephone manner. She was constantly rude to callers without realising it. Basically she was a nervous wreck with a turbulent love life and a growing dependency on marihuana. There was a movie actor in town, just back from Italy and Spain where he had made a Spaghetti Western. I had left a message at his hotel and he called back later in the day. The researcher took the call and gave him pretty short shrift - she had never heard of him.

He had made an impact on TV with his series *Rawhide* but not with her, and now he was branching out into movies. His name was Clint Eastwood. Consequently, *Film Night* missed the opportunity to obtain his first UK interview. I met him several years later when he was a huge star and director. The researcher eventually committed suicide, poor girl.

One of the first movie star interviews I filmed was Glenn Ford who was staying at London's Savoy Hotel - they all seemed to stay there in those days, apart from David Niven who stayed at the Connaught and Alfred Hitchcock who stayed at Claridge's. The hotel kindly provided an area free of charge (now every establishment charges a 'facility fee') and we set up our camera, lights and sound equipment as best we could.

At the appointed hour the Hollywood actor, renowned for his roles in *Gilda, The Blackboard Jungle* and *The Sheepman*, entered and I introduced him to the interviewer Tony

Bilbow. I pointed to the seat we had nominated for him to sit in. He paused for a moment then held his hand to his jaw and said. *I have been having some trouble with a tooth and my face is swollen so - er - I was wondering if I could sit in the opposite seat.* I readily agreed and we spent some minutes readjusting the lighting. He was patient and pleasant and the interview proceeded at a rather slow pace. There was no way anyone could rush Glenn Ford. He was once reported as saying *if they tried to rush me, I'd always say I've only got one other speed, and it's slower.* After the interview he thanked me for being so understanding about his jaw.

In those days, when all interviews outside a TV studio were filmed, you had to wait until the 16mm picture had been processed and synchronised with the sound on magnetic tape. When I eventually viewed the 'rushes' before I started editing the interview, I realised that Glenn Ford looked the same as he always looked in movies - from his left profile. Glenn Ford had had no toothache. He knew which was his 'best side' and made sure he was filmed that way. Who could blame him? Most movie stars are the same.

Although I was *Film Night's* producer, which gave me creative as well as budgetary control of the programme, I was also its director from time to time. I could direct cameras in a studio, although I usually brought in another staff member to do the task on this weekly show but I would often direct film on location. The dividing line between producer and director in TV is less apparent than in movies. So as producer/director I took my camera crew and interviewer to film Alfred Hitchcock one afternoon in his favourite suite at Claridge's Hotel in London.

The door was opened by the chambermaid, a tiny, inoffensive woman with a quiet voice, short hair and a black dress. I was wrong. It was his *wife*, Alma Reville, an editor and screenwriter who had worked with her husband on such classics as *The Thirty Nine Steps*, *The Lady Vanishes*, *Suspicion*,

Shadow of a Doubt and *The Paradine Case*, to name but a few. Appearances can be misleading.

As she ushered us into the room where the interview was to take place, I looked into the bedroom on the right. There was the great man with that great profile and paunch, sound asleep upright in his chair. I have never been able to catnap so have always admired those who can. 'Hitch' was someone who could.

Cables from nearby power points were needed to light the scene. The technician carefully bound them to the floor with tape so that the top-heavy director would not trip as he took his seat for the filming. There was no need to worry, he had been on film sets before, he knew what to expect. He adroitly manoeuvred his way around them and sat down. The interviewer, Sheridan Morley, a big, amiable, bumbling man, even in his late twenties, walked to take his seat. He tripped over them all.

Sir Alfred Hitchcock (he was later knighted) was always an interesting interviewee. I remember him saying *the secret of a good mystery is to tell the audience everything.* He was right, it just had not occurred to me until then. He was renowned for saying that actors were like cattle. During the interview his riposte was *what I probably said was that all actors should be treated like cattle.*

The reply I enjoyed most was when he commented on the fact that his own TV series *Alfred Hitchcock Presents* was *bringing murder back into its rightful setting, the home.* He also explained why, in his thriller *Shadow of a Doubt,* he chose Joseph Cotten as the male lead. *I cast Joseph Cotten because he was a very attractive man, otherwise he could never have lured those women victims.* It was perfect casting.

Although I filmed interviews for *Film Night*, most took place in our tiny Presentation 'B' studio at BBC TV Centre. In the late 1960s and early 70s there were no chat shows on

British TV – Michael Parkinson's interview show came later - so when movie stars were brought to London by film companies to publicise their movies, the only significant national television outlet by now was my BBC2 weekly programme.

By now the *Film Night* slot had moved to Sundays, so each Sunday afternoon we would videotape a star interview and play that segment into the 'live' programme later that evening. Joseph Cotten was an early guest and after his recording, we videotaped an interview with his wife, the British actress Patricia Medina, for future transmission. I knew a stage name when I heard it. I knew Doris Day had been born Doris Kappelhoff. Secretly I wondered about Patricia Medina's *real* name. She had appeared in *The Three Musketeers, Lady in the Iron Mask* and dare I say it, *Abbott and Costello in the Foreign Legion.*

After the interview she asked me if I would call her mother in London to let her know the broadcast date. She gave me the London telephone number and I enquired as politely as I could what was her mother's name? *Mrs. Medina* was her reply!

The section of the Joseph Cotten interview I remember most was when he spoke of making *The Magnificent Ambersons,* Orson Welles' first movie after his highly acclaimed *Citizen Kane* and a hard act to follow. As some of the film took place on a sled in the snow, Welles insisted it be shot in a Los Angeles ice works. This way the actors' hoary breaths would be apparent when they spoke. It was a realistic touch but Cotten said he had never been so cold in his life.

I have other memories of visits by movie stars to *Film Night.* Once when there was an industrial dispute with BBC Scenery Department, no furniture or props could be brought into any studio, not even a chair. That is why Jack Nicholson was interviewed standing up. He made no fuss and even sat casually on the floor until the recording took place.

I had admired Shirley MacLaine's superb peaches and cream complexion in her then latest film *The Bliss of Mrs. Blossom*. When she came into the studio, the red-headed star had a mass of freckles. Why should this disappoint me? She was intelligent, warm and funny, that should have been enough.

The Greek star of *Never on Sunday* Melina Mercouri, came to the studio accompanied by her mother, her sister and other assorted relatives. They all stood in the crowded control room during the recording and provided a running commentary which was rather distracting. Of all the many women who were interviewed on *Film Night*, there were two who were so warm, outgoing and friendly that, after only knowing them for a couple of hours, I leant over and kissed them goodbye - Merlina Mercouri and the voluptuous British actress Diana Dors.

I remember Miss Dors' visit for another reason. Her third husband, a somewhat impecunious actor with a drink problem called Alan Lake, escorted her to the studio, sat in the programme's hospitality suite and drank vodka. When his wife returned, he reverted to orange juice, pleading with us not to tell Diana his secret. As if she didn't know. She died far too young of cancer in 1984. Alan Lake could not live without her so shot himself two years later.

To my mind, the most beautiful actress to be interviewed in the studio was Britt Ekland, at that time the estranged wife of Peter Sellers. She had superb bone structure, flawless skin, an excellent figure and wore a stunning ankle-length lizard-skin coat. It is a pity she was not a good actress.

Almost as beautiful was the English actress Jacqueline Bisset who had made it big in Hollywood. She wore little make-up, always looked a picture of health (her father was a doctor in Surrey) and spoke eloquently.

Not only was Joan Collins beautiful, she was remarkably likeable and very professional. Sitting in the make-up chair, she pulled something out of her rather large handbag. It was the bejewelled top she thought she would wear for the interview and sought my approval. Clutched in her hand it seemed fine. When she put it on it looked wonderful. She *knew* what suited her and as she gets older she looks better and better.

The most intelligent and articulate actress to grace the studio was Diana Rigg. I could listen to her all day - she talks such good sense and offers a jaunty slice of cynicism. Like another British actress Vanessa Redgrave, she is a tall, big-boned woman with strong, piercing eyes and a personality to match. She was promoting a film in which she co-starred with George C. Scott *The Hospital*, a jaundiced look at America's health system, written by that masterful screenwriter Paddy Chayevsky. I shall always remember a line Diana Rigg uttered in the film clip we showed on the programme that day *I was having the obligatory affair with a Hopi Indian at the time.*

Telly Savalas became world-famous when he was chosen to play on US TV the lollipop-sucking New York detective *Kojak* in 1973. The year before that he came to the studio to talk about his movie career. He had been in *The Dirty Dozen,* in the James Bond film *On Her Majesty's Secret Service* and *Pancho Villa*, not one of his best, but one in which he played the title role.

Movie stars are often sent on a promotional tour to publicise a so-so film because it needs the exposure. As TV programme makers we benefited from this because, as well as talking about the movie they are sent to promote, they are more than happy to talk about their past and better exploits. Telly Savalas gave a marvellous interview. He was extremely articulate, his stories were succinct, relevant and funny and he had oodles of charm beneath that bald pate. I was surprised to learn he had been an academic, because the few professors I know cannot tell a decent story, let alone a joke. Telly Savalas went up in my estimation. He was a spontaneous, excellent raconteur.

Three weeks later he was interviewed by ITV's rival programme *Cinema*. I watched it. Every story was exactly the same, word for word - the same gestures, the same pauses. That is why he seemed so spontaneous. I should have known.

I could not but admire Olivia de Havilland. Although she had played Melanie in *Gone With the Wind* and won an Oscar for *The Heiress*, she was now in her mid-fifties and making a dire film in England called *Pope Joan* She did not work on Sundays so agreed to be interviewed about her career. She arrived at 2pm precisely wearing no makeup whatsoever. She then sat under the glaring lights for the makeup artist and hairdresser to assess the situation and also to give the studio engineer time to prepare a lighting plan to make her look her best. She left the studio. Two and a half hours later she returned looking, to coin a phrase, *absolutely fabulous.* She had also brought in a pink Christian Dior dress to be ironed before she wore it. When the rather effete dresser returned to the studio, he announced *that label has been stitched in.* No matter, it was a good interview although Olivia de Havilland, the actress, was always present, never the real person.

I recall that she gave a good example of how movie myths are created erroneously. She said she had been reading for years how she did not get on with her co-star, the glamorous Rita Hayworth, in *The Strawberry Blonde* in 1941. *It was simply not true.* She continued. *Rita has a quiet disposition. When she is sitting on the set, she likes to be quiet. She is not flamboyant, she is not temperamental, she is not a great talker. I sensed this and did not disturb her. So we sat next to one another in the studio in silence. A gossip columnist saw this and reported to the world that we hated each other. That story persists to this day.* However, she did not deny that she and her movie actress sister Joan Fontaine, were not the closest of friends. I do not think George Sanders was very close to his brother Tom Conway, particularly when the latter played 'the Falcon' so successfully in the 40s; Shirley MacLaine tolerates but is not bosom pals with her brother Warren Beatty.

The women in my production team were crazy about Mel Brooks when he came into the studio. He was flavour of the month at the time with his hit Western parody *Blazing Saddles* and was in London to promote it. I was less enamoured of him. His manic behaviour on and off camera irked me. I found him exhausting. Even when he had talked non-stop in the studio during the interview, he came immediately afterwards into the control room and continued his cabaret performance in front of the production team and technical crew. I am sure his late quiet, actress wife, Anne Bancroft, complemented him perfectly. I was glad when he left the building.

Years later, in the 20th Century Fox commissary in Los Angeles, he was having lunch when I was introduced to him again. He was much more relaxed, but then so was I. He was like a happy schoolboy when I quoted to him my favourite scene from his movie *History of the World Part I* (there has never been a Part II) in which a placard states: *To the Orgy. First Served, First Come.*

Tony Curtis is a very likeable man - well he was when he came into the studio almost forty years ago. He was still very good looking with piercing blue eyes, a boy from the Bronx called Bernard Schwarz. I am glad he changed his name. And I am glad his first wife also changed her name from Jeanette Morrison to Janet Leigh. Can you imagine their daughter being called Jamie Morrison Schwarz? She'd never have got that role in *A Fish Called Wanda!*

I was not expecting Tony Curtis to be an easy man to deal with. He had been a huge Hollywood star in such movies as *Sweet Smell of Success, The Defiant Ones, Some Like It Hot,*

Spartacus, The Great Race and *The Boston Strangler*. He was in London making the TV series with Roger Moore *The Persuaders* and agreed to come to the studio one Sunday afternoon to record an interview with Tony Bilbow about his career. His American publicist was the difficult one, not the star. He made all the arrangements on behalf of his client and to justify his enormous salary, he needed us to perceive the star as a temperamental, spoilt child.

If the publicist rang me once in the days preceding the interview, he rang me thirty times. *What kind of a studio will he be in? What size dressing room will he have? What will the interviewer be wearing? What kind of chair will he sit in? How late can we leave it for his arrival - he does not like to be kept waiting?* And so it went on. *Tony Curtis must be a monster,* I surmised. I got a panic call on the morning of the interview from the anxious publicist. *Tony Curtis is very fussy about the type of car he travels in. So what kind of limousine are you sending to collect him?* I had no idea. It was Sunday morning and an associate had made the booking the previous week. I told him I would call back. I duly enquired and he seemed happy when I rang to reassure him it was a large chauffeur-driven vehicle. If he had also asked *what colour,* I would have cancelled the whole shebang.

When Tony Curtis arrived he was affable and easy-going. I am sure if we had sent a black taxi cab to collect him he would not have minded. But that nagging suspicion lurked. *Was Tony Curtis nice because someone else dealt with all the nasty bits?* Perhaps I should not have disliked the publicist so much. During the interview Tony Curtis revealed that in *Some Like It Hot* he impersonated Cary Grant when he played the rich playboy. He then went on to say that his role in *The Boston Strangler* had been the most challenging of his career.

He eulogised about London and British TV, particularly its wild life documentaries. He had had a wild life himself but was now newly married to Lesley and besotted by his baby son. It was all quite endearing. Of course the inevitable happened. He divorced Lesley (or vice versa), married someone else, the son grew up and died young. The last time I saw Tony Curtis was just before Christmas 1989 in the Pan Am First Class lounge at Los Angeles Airport. His hair was dyed too dark, his fading good looks made him look debauched, his clothing was dated and too tight, and he wore a flamboyant flowing cravat. He looked ridiculous.

The horror actor Vincent Price's visit to BBC TV Centre was a wholly different experience. He was a big man with a deep, resonant voice. He was also extremely intelligent, amusingly self-deprecating and a great art collector - for himself and others. He married for the second time late in the Australian-born actress Coral Browne, who had had a reputation in London for her bawdy language and outrageous behaviour. They seemed a mismatched pair but appearances can be deceptive, perhaps he tamed her. He was a marvellous raconteur and of the fund of stories he told to the cameras, this was my favourite.

I never go to previews of my movies. I wait until they have been playing for a couple of weeks, then sneak into the back row of a suburban cinema to judge the local audience's reaction. On this particular day, I entered after the movie had begun and found myself sitting next to a woman who was completely involved with what was going on up on the big screen. As the story became scarier and scarier, she instinctively grabbed the sleeve of the person sitting next to her. She held it tighter and tighter. At a crucial moment, when she was so frightened she could no longer look at the screen, she shared that moment with the person beside her whose arm she had grabbed. She took one look at my face - and screamed. I left immediately.

I worked extremely hard on *Film Night*. I was expected to produce fifty ½ hour programmes per year. I had to be well organised because not all editions could be transmitted 'live'. My small team and I needed a summer and a Christmas break so I used to pre-record several future programmes, usually choosing a specific topic and calling it *A Film Night Special*. This had to be done in the same week as I produced a regular 'live' programme. It became particularly hectic towards Christmas. I was at my wit's end to get everything finished on time and my concentration occasionally wavered.

One year, a few days before Christmas, I had to dash over to a tiny screening room (one of several) in the East Tower of BBC TV Centre to view urgently a 16mm print of an edited location report. As I arrived at the door of my screening room I noticed a familiar face several yards away outside a nearby screening room. She was small and pretty with gently-waved hair and was wearing a dark patterned woollen skirt and knee-length boots. Her face was familiar but I could not place her. Who was she? I racked my brain, to no avail.

Then a tall, erect man came and stood beside her. It was the Duke of Edinburgh. The hatless woman waiting there was The Queen. They had each driven themselves in separate cars and she had arrived informally a few minutes before her husband. As I went in to my screening room, they went to theirs. It was a preview of that year's Christmas Day Broadcast. It must have met with their approval because, when I left my screening room, the place was empty.

Nine

A Date With Ryan's Daughter

As *Film Night* became more successful so the occasional overseas filming trip became possible. In those days I never had to worry too much about my programme budget. The BBC was flush with cash in those days as millions of viewers traded their black-and-white sets for colour and paid the higher licence fee. So I spent what was needed without being profligate and nobody complained. When I asked if I could film overseas, as long as I had a good reason for doing so, I went.

The first was to Ireland where the Oscar-winning director David Lean was making *Ryan's Daughter*. Set in 1916, it tells of a young woman in western Ireland who marries a local schoolteacher then has an affair with a British officer stationed in the town. The screenplay was written by Robert Bolt (*Lawrence of Arabia, Doctor Zhivago, A Man for All Seasons* etc.) and the stars were Robert Mitchum, Sarah Miles (Bolt's then-wife), Trevor Howard, John Mills, Leo McKern and Christopher Jones.

The cinematographer was Freddie Young, who like Bolt had worked on Lean's previous Oscar-winning epics. We were promised interviews with all of them, except Christopher Jones who was 'difficult'. It turned out that MGM thought he would be the new James Dean after he had appeared in the film *Three in the Attic* but he could barely act and was practically inarticulate. In the finished film his voice was dubbed by the English actor Julian Holloway. I was unaware of these failings but not too disheartened by missing out on only one interview. This would be a week to remember.

We flew to Shannon in Western Ireland. Our TV team comprised Tony Bilbow the interviewer, Irene Beach the producer's assistant, a lighting cameraman and his assistant, a sound operator and his assistant, and me. We collected two hire cars, one for the production team, one for the crew, and set off. Tony drove the production car. He is the driver from hell. In life, he is aware of few things going on around him, women excepted. In a car this is not good. Ireland is remarkably pretty and green. At that time there were not too many cars on the road and Tony drove too fast in such a sleepy part of the country. I wondered what the farmers thought as they passed in their horse-drawn drays full of peat and waved. I did not need to wonder what a small child thought as she was nearly mowed down by Tony, saved by a last-minute swerve.

We stopped at one of those tea rooms where the hospitality overwhelms you. It is an art the Irish have acquired over centuries. They have the gift of the gab too, a natural lyricism which is most appealing. These hard-working ladies served us large pots of freshly-brewed tea, mountains of sandwiches and scones and jam and cakes and then charged a pittance. After that comfort stop, Irene was unwilling to venture further in the production car and switched to the other vehicle with a sensible driver. A few years later she married one of the passengers, the sound assistant, David, and became Irene Hahn. Something good comes out of everything.

The film location was outside Dingle, on the craggy coastline battered by winds whipping in from the Atlantic. The houses winding along that cobbled street looked authentic because they were built more solidly than the usual plaster and hardboard. Most of them had no interiors, supported instead from behind by tall wooden posts. On the pretty hill behind the false town, David Lean had insisted a dirt road be built. It was never used, it just made a better picture in wide shot.

The inhabitants of these inadequate houses were extras from Tralee. They were bussed in each day, given a hot lunch and received a daily fee. They had never had it so good. All they had to do was dress in period costume and stand outside their houses - and wait. The motto was: *hurry up and wait.* David Lean did not shoot one foot of film until the weather was just as he wanted it and until every extra was in exactly the right position. I saw him looking through the camera viewfinder and instructing his assistant director (David never raised his voice) to move a woman outside one particular building a few inches to the left, a child outside another house a foot or two further down the road. And so it went on until the shot had been composed like an oil painting. His attention to detail was astonishing. That is how classic films are made.

This movie was being shot on 70mm, twice the gauge of the usual feature film. Lean and his cinematographer were determined it was going to look as good and as clear and as crisp as it could be. I got chatting to the extras standing by their makeshift houses. They invited me inside like good hospitable colleens but of course there was little to see, just curtains and wooden supports. It was charmingly eerie.

Although interviews were promised, to find a suitable moment to take an actor away from the set to visit our tiny 16mm camera set-up nearby, was a nightmare. As the days passed I was constantly worried that I would return to London with very little in the can. To illustrate each interview one needs to edit in some footage shot on location. There was a limit to how much of it I could shoot. The director worked so slowly that it took nearly the entire week of our visit to film one complex scene in that village street, a scene which would last only a few minutes in the finished film. In the real town of Dingle nearby, there was a viewing area in the local church hall and dubbing facilities for post-synchronising dialogue. Outside, sheep wandered aimlessly along and making their presence felt with the occasional bleat.

The town became famous. Robert Mitchum took over a large mansion as his living quarters. Rumour had it that one evening two London girls, who had met the actor there en route to Ireland, arrived in Dingle unannounced. When the actor was informed of their presence, he simply said *put them in rooms 12 and 14*. When he tired of their company he sent them back to London and summoned his wife in Los Angeles to join him. And so it went on for nearly a year.

Mitchum eventually agreed under pressure to be filmed by us. This was a BBC2 programme and Tony Bilbow tried to conduct an intelligent interview. Mitchum sent the whole thing up by making amusing, sarcastic comments which were patently untrue. After about 7 minutes, Bilbow gave up, ending with the usual *Robert Mitchum, thank you*. It is then that the director usually calls *cut*. For some inexplicable reason I did not say anything and the camera kept rolling.

Once Mitchum thought the interview was over, he relaxed and was quite amusing. He told an anecdote about when he started in movies as a contract screen writer for one of the big studios. He tried to do as little writing as possible - his laconic manner dictated that. A more experienced colleague told him always to wear a hat to work. So each day Mitchum would hang his hat on the office rack and go out to chat up starlets or go on a drinking spree. If anyone rang the office to ask where he was, someone would always reply *well, he's around somewhere because his hat is on a peg in his office*. That would suffice. That story formed the basis of the transmitted interview. From then on I was always reluctant to call *cut*.

Years later when I was working on BBC1 with another presenter Barry Norman, I arranged for him to go on location just outside London where Robert Mitchum was starring in a remake of *The Big Sleep* directed by Michael Winner. The TV crew set up and waited. Barry filmed interviews with Winner and another of the film's stars Oliver Reed, who, contrary to rumour, was very professional on set. They then hung around for the rest of the day to get the all-important Mitchum interview in the can.

Barry became more irritated until he was promised that at the end of the day's shooting Mitchum would be available. He did not keep his promise - at 5.45pm a car drove by. The actor sneered and shoved two fingers at Barry and the crew. Not a nice man. Yet the Assistant Director on *Ryan's Daughter*, Roy Stevens, told me he was very fond of Mitchum, even though he had spent a night in an Irish jail on his behalf. After Mitchum had left the rented mansion in Dingle, it was discovered that the greenhouse was full of marijuana plants!

Sarah Miles wanted to be co-operative and we set up her interview in an unwanted part of that day's movie set-up, the farmyard. She was highly-strung and to overcome this and her inherent shyness, she started to show off and say outrageous things she did not really mean. It made the interview fun. During it, when the nearby fowl were at their loudest, she stopped and said *piss off chickens*. It was wonderfully timed. Tony Bilbow and I were pleased with her spontaneity and intelligent responses to his questioning.

On our return to TV Centre, the interview was edited and its transmission date announced in the press. As I've mentioned, *Film Night* was transmitted 'live' each Sunday evening with filmed excerpts when necessary. On the morning of the broadcast I was at home when the phone rang. It was Robert

Bolt, the award-winning screenwriter. Why did he need to call *me*? He pleaded with me not to broadcast the scheduled interview with his wife. He explained she was overwrought at the time and now she was deeply worried about how she would be perceived if it were broadcast. Eventually I assured him that the more excessive moments had been removed and there was nothing to worry about. That must have calmed Sarah down and I heard no more from them, even though that one line remained - *piss off chickens.*

John Mills played a mute in the movie and won Best Supporting Actor Oscar for his portrayal, a non-speaking role too. What he had to say in the interview was more than adequate and he explained succinctly how a special mouth plate was used to distort his face; and how his hair achieved its 'village idiot' cut. As he was 'on call' every day we were there we had to interview him dressed for the part but without the false teeth. It was an incongruous experience. He was dressed like a fool and spoke like an aristocrat.

The cinematographer Freddie Young later told me that during the storm sequence being filmed at the exposed Ennis Peninsular, John Mills nearly drowned when his boat capsized. When he realised he was going to be thrown into the water, John took out his teeth and stuffed them in his pocket so that they would not be lost. The makeup man who had designed the special plate was much relieved.

Trevor Howard, with that cut-glass English accent, played a heavy-drinking Irish priest in the movie. To interview him in costume minus the Irish accent, also seemed strange. By this time he had been working on location for *Ryan's Daughter* for several months and had had enough, simply because he had to wear three days' growth of beard at all times. Until then I did not realise that continuity in a David Lean movie could ruin an actor's love life for months. Perhaps Mrs. Howard liked designer stubble before it became fashionable.

Freddie Young was so exhausted at the end of a day behind the camera that when we interviewed him he could not remember the names of the other David Lean movies he had worked on. It was a very short interview. To be fair, he was 68 at the time and working arduously and assiduously on location in all kinds of weather, for months on end. He really did not retire until he was nearly 90.

I met him at lunch and dinner parties several times in London until his death in 1998 at the age of 96. His reminiscences were fascinating. After all, he was the cameraman on *49th Parallel* way back in 1941, his first collaboration with Lean. He respected the director enormously but I sensed Freddie was well aware of the talented director's egoism and vanity.

It was important that the week's filming culminated with an interview with the great director himself. He was a good looking man and although well into middle age, he was most attractive to the opposite sex. His travelling companion during the long shoot in County Kerry was a tall, elegant blonde. I saw them together in the evenings at the Great Southern Hotel in Killarney where we all stayed. She eventually became Mrs. David Lean although there were several before her, one being the star of *The Seventh Veil*, Ann Todd, who later produced and directed travel films after her huge divorce settlement.

In Ireland David Lean was so immersed in his 70mm movie that it became more and more apparent that the promised BBC interview would not take place. On the second last day of our stay we were driving back from the set rather forlornly when a Rolls Royce passed us on this tiny country road. It stopped twenty yards along and out stepped the maestro himself. *You will get your interview all right - at the schoolhouse at 5 o'clock tomorrow evening.* Having avoided us for most of the week, I was still not convinced he would turn up.

We arrived at the location, an authentic stone schoolhouse built especially for the movie but unused that day. The BBC cameraman could not believe his eyes. In chalk on the floor was Freddie Young's lighting plan for the interview. The good-looking David Lean wanted to look his best and wanted to ensure that his own cinematographer was indirectly responsible for the lighting. No doubt he gained thousands more female admirers when the interview was shown on *Film Night.*

What I liked about the interview was the way Lean embraced his passion for film. He said he loved even the smell and feel of actual film. He loved passing it through his fingers as he proceeded to edit his epics. He had started life as a film editor which he said prepared him well for his later career as a director. He knew instinctively where a shot he was filming would end, how it would be linked to the next shot and how effective it would be. He liked a movie to tell the story in pictures without dialogue for as long as possible. And he wanted each shot in its own right to be like a masterpiece painting.

When you view his considerable body of work you realise he practised what he preached. Even when we were filming for television the setting up of a general rehearsal shot in that Irish movie street he had created, he looked deeply contemplative as he accidentally came into our shot which is exactly what we wanted. Out of the corner of his eye he must have noticed the camera and instinctively walked towards it, then out to the left of the frame, simply to provide an ideal editing point. I was most grateful. He really knew his craft.

The week's filming was over. Apart from the irksome Robert Mitchum experience, it had been a successful outing. It was Saturday and we were heading for home. Our luggage was put in the larger crew car and Irene travelled with them. I wished I could have done so too but, as producer, I could not leave the interviewer to drive alone to the airport. It was with some foreboding that I stepped into the passenger seat and waved goodbye to the others as they sped off on the long drive back to Shannon Airport.

It was typical Irish weather, dull with drizzling rain. Tony seemed to drive a little slower than I had remembered on the trip out, but he never slowed down as we went round bends. Just outside Limerick, he tore around a sharp corner and the car started to skid on the wet road. I knew I was experiencing my first car accident. Everything seemed to happen in slow motion. These were my thoughts in the few seconds it all happened:

Oh we are skidding across the road. Thank goodness there's nothing coming the other way. Oh we are going through a fence. And now we are heading towards a plough in the field.

And that is where we landed, up against a farmer's old plough. The front of the car was a wreck. Although I was in the passenger seat, I was unscathed but Tony needed several stitches in his head. After treatment, we were driven back to Shannon Airport, having missed the flight. Our luggage had gone ahead. I went up to the Hertz car rental desk to report the accident and gave a hazy description of a field in a farm near Limerick where they might find the damaged car in order to retrieve it. I have never heard from that day to this whether they ever did.

Ten   The Italian Job

I was quite excited when the *Film Night* researcher, Sheldon Larry, had arranged an interview with Dirk Bogarde in Rome. The actor lived in France and had never been a studio guest at BBC TV Centre, like many of his British contemporaries. We also knew that David Niven would be in the city at the same time so we arranged to film him too. To justify the expense of the trip, we needed to line up more interviews. Sheldon was brilliant. He persuaded three great Italian directors to participate. All spoke good English. When I look back and realise that in one week, I went to the houses of Franco Zeffirelli, Pier Paulo Pasolini and Luchino Visconti, I cannot believe my luck. This time only the production team flew to the capital. We hired Umberto, an Italian cameraman who spoke English with an Australian accent. He brought along his own sound assistant, a Hungarian woman who spoke Italian but no English. They were probably lovers. Umberto helped me understand Italian traffic rules.

Umberto, I said, *these zebra crossings, are they the same as in London?*

Exactly the same, he replied.

But does the traffic stop to let pedestrians cross?

Of course not.

Umberto also tried to enlighten me about Italian politics. I knew the gag about the man who had a full time job as group photographer for the Italian government, but he went further.

Our government has a terrible time trying to raise money. You see, many irresponsible Italians do not pay taxes. It is bankrupting the country.

That's a dreadful state of affairs, I responded, *what kind of Italians behave like that?*

People like me, for instance, he muttered without one iota of remorse. No wonder he had returned to Rome, having emigrated to Melbourne six years earlier.

When it came to filming interviews, Umberto was the true professional. We found a good location at Dirk Bogarde's hotel, The Hassler, just above the Spanish Steps for the first interview. There is no doubt about it, Bogarde was an intelligent, articulate man but he didn't fool me. He *acted* the story of his life and career and a waspish tone intruded upon whatever he said. While all he said on camera was good value for broadcasting, I never found him endearing and rarely self-deprecating. He was a bitter man.

When I met him in 1970 he was approaching 50. He was still good looking and dapper, but shorter and smaller than I had imagined. He was full of praise for the work he was now doing with Visconti. He had just made *The Damned* and praised the visual flair of the director and the sumptuous and colourful settings he created, often with judicious lighting effects. Reviewers did not like the movie one bit. One critic thought it was like watching an opera without the score. I was on Dirk's side.

He went on to say that the disciplines he had learned during his British movie career proved useful making an Italian movie. The self-indulgent Visconti, who had mostly worked with European actors, was not used to such professionalism. In *The Damned* Dirk had to make an important after-dinner speech to the family of German industrialists. Only the wide shot and close-ups of the dinner and guests had been filmed when it was time to pack up for the day. Visconti was worried about the expense of re-hiring the dinner guest actors for an extra day while Dirk made his speech. Dirk told Visconti not to be concerned. The next day he made the speech in close-up to an empty table - in one take. He was trained to do that.

Bogarde had fond memories of working with Joseph Losey in *The Servant, King and Country* and *Accident;* also with John Schlesinger in *Darling* but he was quite scathing about his days as a featured player for The Rank Organisation and the mindless *Doctor* films. I thought he should have been more charitable towards his former employer as these movies had made him a household name. If he had had a higher regard for his fans, I'd have liked him more. After all it was Rank who had financed his most controversial film, *Victim,* about a barrister with homosexual leanings who tried to confront the gang of blackmailers who had caused the death of his best friend, despite the risk to his own reputation. Deep down, Bogarde was rightly proud of this film for it led indirectly to his later, successful associations with Losey, and Visconti. It also seemed to me that during our interview with the star, he enjoyed explaining that he had turned his back on Britain because no one offered him prestigious roles any more.

When British actors make films overseas they invariably crave for the company of fellow countrymen. I noticed this often during my TV career and Dirk Bogarde was no exception. Nevertheless, it was very generous of him to invite the interviewer, Tony Bilbow, and the production team to dinner that evening at his favourite ristorante. We dined outside in the warm spring air and Dirk regaled us with wonderful stories. He told us about Dame Edith Evans. When she had been in Rome the previous week to recite a poem outside St. Peter's for a TV programme, the crew was not allowed to film her until all the tourists had left the Vatican for the day. A couple of hours later, shortly after 9pm, Dirk decided to wander down to watch the tail end of the filming and renew his friendship with the grand lady of British theatre, then take her out for a bite to eat. When he arrived the place was in darkness. He wondered if he had written the wrong date in his diary. He made some enquiries and discovered that Dame Edith and the crew had left ages ago. She had recited the poem in one take - at the age of 72. When they did meet the following day, he told her about his new car.

I've got a new car, too, announced the actress.

What kind is it? Dirk enquired.

Black she replied.

He learned later it was a Rolls Royce.

The evening was a lot of fun and Irene, my assistant, sat there opposite Dirk Bogarde, thinking her parents back in London would never believe her. I was irritated when he started talking about *The Servant* and threw in the casual remark *I was engaged to Sarah Miles at the time*. Why did he have to say that? Sitting right next to him as he spoke was Tony Forwood, who had left his actress wife, Glynis Johns and young child, to start a long-term relationship with Dirk. It was obviously a committed partnership. Tony looked after Dirk like a mother rooster. When the restaurant bill came, Tony paid it discreetly. I am sure Dirk never carried money, Tony looked after everything. They had a beautiful villa near Grasse and a lovely car which only Tony drove. Here was Dirk pretending to us in front of us that his male partner was only his manager. Years later Bogarde became a best-selling author although I still detected that irritating, waspish tone in his writing. Once again what irked me more were those casual references to his "manager".

In 1983, Dirk Bogarde gave a *Guardian Lecture,* really an interview, at London's National Film Theatre, which was filmed for BBC2. I was the Executive Producer. When I met him again, I noticed he was smaller, frailer and just as bitter about life. I did not remind him of the lovely dinner we had had together in Rome in 1970. Nor did I mention one of the most interesting press conferences I had ever attended, thanks to him.

At the end of dinner on that balmy evening in Rome, Dirk casually invited Tony Bilbow, Sheldon Larry, Irene Beach and me to an announcement the following morning about his forthcoming film. When we entered the building on the dot of eleven, Dirk rushed forward and said *Irene, how nice to see you again.* He went on to greet us individually by name. That was the actor at his charming best. It was most impressive. I recognised from newspaper photographs that the man seated on the platform was the director, Luchino Visconti whom we were to interview later in the week. With him was a beautiful slim, blond Swedish teenage boy. He was introduced as Bjorn Andresen. His equally stunning grandmother was his chaperone.

That was how we learned about the proposed filming of *Death in Venice* in which Bogarde later gave the performance of his career and Bjorn played the elusive Tadzio. Based on the Thomas Mann novella, it dealt with latent homosexuality as much as old age and death. Visconti explained to the assembled crowd how he wished to cloak Venice in fog but knew it would be difficult to obtain permission. When I saw the finished film, I wondered how many million lira had changed hands to achieve that. Or had he been lucky with the weather? The result was stunning, Venice at its best. At that press conference, Visconti mentioned that Mahler's music would be featured prominently on the soundtrack.

As a result, the adagio from his 5th Symphony has become a world wide hit.

The next interview to be filmed was with Franco Zeffirelli who had had a great box office success with his sumptuous version of Shakespeare's *Romeo and Juliet*. It starred two unknowns, Leonard Whiting and Olivia Hussey. Fame is so transitory. Who remembers Leonard Whiting now? He made his last movie in 1971 at the ripe old age of 21. Zeffirelli had also made a film version of *The Taming of the Shrew* with Elizabeth Taylor and Richard Burton, so those two movies were all we had to talk about. But it was interesting to see how his experience as an opera director influenced his approach to film. He was so charming with his blond, patrician good looks that anything he said with his delightful Italian accent would suffice.

What I remember most about our visit to his villa on the outskirts of Rome was the cinema projection booth he had built behind his spacious and gracious living room, just like a Hollywood mogul.

From there we moved to an apartment in a suburb of Rome where the noted director Pier Paulo Pasolini lived. He was a quiet intellectual with strong Marxist views, and very polite. His home was simple but bourgeois in its decor. I needed to use his bathroom and I am almost certain there was a twee cover over the spare toilet roll. He left that side of things to his housekeeper. He had recently completed filming *Medea* starring the opera singer Maria Callas and he was fulsome in his praise of her as a screen actress. Despite that, it was her first and last screen appearance.

Pasolini was about to film *Decameron* followed by Chaucer's *Canterbury Tales* which was to be shot in England. It was a difficult interview as all his replies were in Italian. He understood English perfectly and spoke it quite well, but he wanted to reply in his native tongue. For all I knew, Pasolini's answers could have been as inappropriate as

Robert Mitchum's, but on our return to the UK a translator got to work and what he had to say was erudite, pertinent and boring.

As far as I could see, the man had little warmth and no sense of humour. The overt sexuality which dominated aspects of his movies was wholly unapparent in the man himself. He was a gentle soul and I liked him. It was incongruous to me that he should die so violently five years later. Rumours persist about what really happened but it is thought a former boyfriend ran the wheels of Pasolini's own car several times over the director's body in a park on the outskirts of the city. He did not deserve that fate.

There could not be two more different personalities than Pasolini and Visconti. We had seen Visconti briefly at the press conference but had not met him. This was to be Tony Bilbow's final interview before his early return to London. We went to Visconti's magnificent villa - he was, after all, a Count - where we were ushered in to a sumptuous room, rather green and somewhat dark but furnished with precious antiques in exquisite taste. Visconti welcomed us politely but I found him rather sinister. I cannot tell you why, it was a feeling I had. I had seen his magnificent Royal Opera production of *Il Trovatore* at Covent Garden some years earlier and I knew some of his movies, *Rocco and His Brothers, The Leopard and The Damned* so I knew he was a man of great style.

With Visconti in the room on this occasion was a woman friend who was also a screenwriter - Nicola Bandalucco and they had just completed the screenplay together for *Death in Venice*. I was nervous the whole time I was at Visconti's house because I knew we had only one 400-foot roll of 16mm film left, just under 10 minutes, which is not long for a filmed interview before it is edited. We had brought our own film stock from London earlier in the week and it was running out. We had contacted BBC London to send more but to my chagrin it had not yet arrived. To acquire the necessary extra film stock in Rome in those days would have been a bureaucratic nightmare. Tony Bilbow began the interview aware of the problem. He managed to end it just before we ran out of film. I was so grateful. It was long enough.

Our interviewer had radio commitments back in London so Irene had booked him on the only Friday early morning flight available to enable Tony to get to the BBC studio on time. He was a nervous traveller so Irene withheld from him the name of the airline. She just handed him his ticket and told him the check-in time. After our return a few days later, Tony came into the production office and said. *You won't believe this, but I flew back from Rome with Air Zambia.* Both Irene and I tried to look surprised.

There was one more interview to film in Rome - David Niven. As Tony had returned to London, I was the interviewer. I was nervous of this great star before I met him. I knew he would be urbane, debonair, oozing confidence and joie de vivre. How would he react to an Australian interviewer who wasn't really much of an interviewer at all? This is the day I would be found out; my lack of talent would be revealed. This made me even more nervous as I prepared my questions as best I could.

We found a location with views of Rome in the background. David Niven appeared alone and without an entourage. He was just what I had expected - a 6' 1" tall, good looking, slim, 60 year old Englishman and utterly charming. He put me at my ease straight away. It is usually the other way round. The interview proceeded - by now the extra film stock had arrived - and all went well for the first 10 minutes when the film ran out and the camera had to be reloaded. He was a wonderful raconteur as we would learn later when he wrote his two volumes of autobiography.

The interview, to my mind, was going extremely well. David Niven turned to me, looking rather glum. He was upset that he wasn't giving a very good performance. He needed reassurance. *Am I doing all right? I am happy to start the interview all over again, if you wish. I am not telling those stories very well, am I? Can you understand what I am saying?* I could not believe my ears. Here was an excellent interviewee and here he was full of self-doubt. Here was the actor who was such a persuasive jewel thief in *Raffles*, a magnificent Fritz von Tarlenheim to Ronald Colman's Ruritanian King in *Prisoner of Zenda,* a brave World War I pilot in *Dawn Patrol,* a dashing British cavalryman in *Charge of the Light Brigade* and an ideal Phileas Fogg in *Around the World in 80 Days.* Here he was in Rome feeling troubled and tentative as David Niven.

He told wonderful stories of how he had started in Hollywood as an extra, playing a Mexican in a sombrero; how he had shared an apartment nicknamed *Cirrhosis-by-the-Sea* with Errol Flynn which resulted in amazing sexual capers with starlets and others; and how proud but undeserving he had felt about winning an Oscar for his role as a supposed war hero in *Separate Tables* in 1958. Now he was off to make his next movie, *The Statue.* It was difficult for him to explain the plot. He was to play a professor with a sculptress wife who makes a statue of him with an enormous male member belonging to someone else. It was a dire movie.

I met David Niven twice more when he came to the BBC TV Centre to be interviewed. By now he was even more famous as the author of the best-selling *The Moon Is A Balloon* and its sequel *Bring on the Empty Horses,* yet he was as unsure and self-effacing as ever. He told an anecdote about the night before filming began on *Death on the Nile.* Peter Ustinov, who was to play Inspector Poirot, invited Niven for a nightcap. He declined. He had a scene the next day with Bette Davis. He had never appeared in a movie with her but his friend Errol Flynn, had warned him years ago about her attitude on the set. She always knew her lines and demanded that everyone else be as competent as she. Niven was determined to have an early night; to learn his lines thoroughly before he went to sleep. He told me he then slept fitfully, anticipating the worst when filming began in the morning. He was extremely surprised when Bette Davis fluffed her lines on the first take. Then she made her confession. *I was so nervous about filming with David Niven, that I hardly slept a wink trying to learn my lines!* He told it more amusingly than that. He was a delightful man, yet he lacked self confidence.

Perhaps he was aware that he had made many movies for the wrong reason - he needed the money. Perhaps he never got over the death of his 28 year old first wife, Primula Rollo, who fell down the stairs at a Hollywood party at the home of Tyrone Power and his wife Annabella, leaving him with two young sons to bring up, one of whom was barely seven months old.

Despite his self doubt, he made a most amusing contribution to the Errol Flynn documentary in *The Hollywood Greats* series Barry Norman and I made in 1977. Off camera at that time he expressed his concern over the health of his great pal, Laurence Olivier who was barely able to speak. As it happened, Olivier outlived him. David Niven developed the dreaded motor neurone disease and died in Switzerland in 1983. His second wife Hjordis was at their home in the South of France at the time

I was honoured to be invited to his Memorial Service at St Martins-in-the-Fields in London's Trafalgar Square. I did not think it necessary to arrive early. As I was walking up the church steps, the photographers suddenly put their cameras and flash bulbs to 'ready'. This was my moment of glory. It was not to be. Right behind me was the Bond actress Joanna Lumley and behind her Lord Snowdon, Princess Margaret's ex-husband.

Inside, one of the ushers, David Frost, suggested I find a seat from the side aisle as the centre aisle seats were full. I went all the way down and could not find anywhere to sit. Then I saw a spare seat. No-one was prepared to move one seat along for me so I steered my way past everybody and sat down. I then realised that I was in the second row, immediately behind Sir Laurence Olivier, who was to deliver the eulogy, and guest of honour Prince Michael of Kent.

But back to Rome. I knew I had a good interview in the can and thanked the actor profusely for his splendid contribution. He was flattered but I doubt whether he believed me. On the plane journey home I reflected again on my good fortune. In one week, apart from meeting two great British actors, Dirk Bogarde and David Niven, I had filmed three great Italian directors.

The following year I added another famous Italian director to my list. Vittoria De Sica came to London to promote *The Garden of the Finzi-Continis*. I went to the Inn on the Park Hotel where the publicist Fred Hift had arranged the interview to take place. There was not much room but the crew and interviewer squeezed in and filming started. Having been an actor as well as a director, De Sica was charming, but was having difficulty speaking English in these restricted and unfamiliar surroundings. He had spoken about his best known film *Bicycle Thieves* in 1948, about directing Sophia Loren in her Oscar-winning performance in *Two Women* in 1961 and his acting role in *Shoes of the Fisherman* in 1968.

He was about to elaborate on his latest film, when the phone rang. Fred Hift took the call and we had to stop filming. When we continued, De Sica had lost his flow and the most important section of the chat was less than satisfactory. I was furious. The next day I wrote an angry letter to the publicist citing his unprofessional behaviour. He wrote an equally angry letter back to me and as a result we became firm friends which lasted until Fred returned to live in New York. Life often works out that way.

I had only one more well-known Italian director to meet and in 1973 it happened. The other *Film Night* presenter, Philip Jenkinson, and I flew to Rome to film Federico Fellini at the famous Cinecitta Studios, an architectural reminder of the Mussolini era. The entrance was a monument to fascism, a typical 1930s building. In his office with kitchen beside it where he could cook pasta to his heart's content, Fellini was, as expected, larger than life. His English was good but he preferred to talk in Italian, a more flamboyant language. And he made the most of it. He rolled his 'r's and emphasised his 's's to dramatic effect. The cameraman could not stay in close-up for long, so wild were his gestures. It was a tour de force from the director of such exotic movies as *La Dolce Vita, 8 ½, Juliet of the Spirits,* and *Satyricon.* You could not but warm to such a big personality. He liked to shock and he filled his films with outrageous-looking extras, chosen from books of photographs he had stacked on his shelves.

To him, what was most important was how his films 'looked'. What people 'said' was far less so. In Italy it is usual for movies to be shot without sound. Therefore the placing of the microphone boom does not inhibit what a director wants to shoot. Philip challenged him on this technique. Fellini brushed him aside saying that if you want an actor to say more words during the dubbing process than he had spoken on the set, you let him say what is needed to be said, and if a few more words spill out after the lips have closed, so what? He then grinned cheekily. He liked to shock.

When we had finished filming, Fellini himself took us down to the studio floor where a huge 1930s passenger steamer had been painted on to the wall of the swimming pool for his latest movie, *Amacord.* The ship looked magnificent standing by the quayside. The bow was tall and elongated and the aft was smaller. Fellini knew all the tricks of perspective. It would look huge on the cinema screen. It looked ready to set sail but was immobile. He explained how a system of tubes and pumps would simulate the ship's wake. Rather naively I asked, *how will you get the ship to leave the dock?* His obvious reply was, *we move the camera, not the ship.* He was not fazed by such an inane question from a TV producer/director who should have known better. That is what I call *a nice man*.

As we left the Cinecitta Studios we passed through an authentic Western set, no doubt used in innumerable Spaghetti Westerns which had been swamping the market at that time. Then came a sorry sight. Rows and rows of people lay in awkward positions in a nearby shed. They were the leftover 'extras' from Michael Winner's film *The Games,* a story about four athletes as they prepared for the gruelling 26 mile marathon in the Olympics.

The final scenes from the movie were set in an Olympic Stadium. The stands had to be full to be effective. There was no way Winner would be a loser. He hired a minimum of extras to be dotted around the arena and filled the rest of the stadium with rows of plastic people. These folk, having done their job, were left to perish among the studio props. What a way to go? They weren't bio-degradable. For all I know their distorted bodies could still be lying there.

In England I filmed an interview with the actor Marcello Mastroianni, he who knew more about film lighting than any Hollywood actress. Like David Lean he arranged for the movie's cinematographer to light the interview set - he was not going to relegate that task to a BBC TV cameraman. Mastroianni's co-star on that movie was Virna Lisa, a prima donna if ever I saw one. As she sat forlornly beside the set, she had her language coach massage her legs and ankles. I bet that was not in the latter's contract but the actress did not care. She needed to be pampered and, from what I could see, ordered minions to cosset her.

The two Italians actors were making an Italian film in England. We were only interested in the male star, who had a higher profile with British moviegoers. Miss Lisi had appeared in *The Secret of Santa Vittoria* with Anthony Quinn and she had also co-starred with David Niven in the ill-fated

The Statue. On this occasion she could not bear the thought that handsome Marcello was getting all the attention. The interview with Mastroianni went well and we were about to pack up to leave when I was approached by a flustered publicist. Would we interview the actress as well?

On camera she was sweetness itself, co-operative and disarmingly nervous because she had been ignored. In most cases, movie stars and directors have always been courteous and pleasant to me. I rarely encountered temper tantrums or outright animosity. Why? I gave them an outlet to publicise themselves. They would be watched by millions who would judge them accordingly. For example, people who have worked with the above-mentioned Michael Winner have told me how difficult and unreasonable he is. I can honestly say I have always found him pleasant, charming and funny because I promoted his movies and his career. He is an interesting, articulate man with an outrageous personality.

I was excited when I flew with the new *Film Night* presenter, Sheridan Morley, to Munich to film an interview with the Italian sex symbol, Gina Lollobrigida. She was a big international movie star, much better known than Virna Lisi, with such Hollywood blockbusters as *Trapeze, Solomon and Sheba* and *Buona Sera, Mrs Campbell* to her credit. Now she was holed up at the Bavarian film studios working on *King, Queen, Knave*. For our visit, I had lined up interviews with the said Miss Lollobrigida, the Polish director Jerzy Skolimowski and the young British actor John Moulder Brown.

We stayed overnight in order to arrive at the studios early the next morning. In the hotel bathroom, whose lighting was far superior to mine at home, I noticed one long hair growing from the top of my nose, just below the brow. I needed a pair of tweezers. No way was the tall Italian star going to be besotted over me if I had a conspicuous growth in the wrong place. I had no tweezers so shaved off that one hair with my razor. The blood started pouring out from that vulnerable part of my anatomy. It would not stop. It flowed and flowed and I was late for the studio. That is how I met Gina Lollobrigida - with a piece of sticking plaster over my nose.

We were allocated a spare dressing room to set up the 16mm camera and lighting. Shortly after our arrival, I saw a tiny woman waddle by in a pink satin dressing gown. She looked casually into the room as she passed. Although no more than 5ft tall she had a large head and big brown eyes. Goodness, it was the star herself. I had only seen her 60ft high, filling a huge cinema screen with her voluptuous body and large bosom. She *had* to be tall. She was not. But she was a flirt and I liked that, despite my head wound. She was a true lady. She never asked me about my nose.

Four years later in Basle, Switzerland, I filmed an interview with Italy's most famous star of all, Sophia Loren. This was with Barry Norman for the weekly BBC 1 programme *Film 76*. At that time I had never seen Miss Loren interviewed on British TV so it was quite a scoop. The film was *The Cassandra Crossing*.

The scene being filmed was to feature Miss Loren boarding a transcontinental train just as it pulled away from Basle railway station, supposedly Geneva. This was a disaster movie, in vogue at the time. It was also an Italian/British/German co-production, a common occurrence in those days, and the director was Greek, George Pan Cosmatos. It was a disaster for me personally, never mind the movie. I get palpitations just thinking about the experience. The big mistake I made was to accept the offer of an American TV crew who were filming a documentary about the making of the movie for the producers, to film the Sophia Loren interview for us, thus saving air fares and accommodation for a BBC crew. What I did not know until I arrived on set was that the movie crew was Italian and that every time the

American TV crew needed any lighting, it was done by the Italians, when available.

The New York cameraman was very obliging and shot for me some location footage of the movie crew at work on the railway station and shots of the actors waiting around or rehearsing their scenes, including Sophia Loren rushing on to the train. OK I had enough footage. I needed to get the interview set up so that the actress could be filmed by us when she had finished her scene. I chose a railway carriage away from the hustle and bustle of the station but not too far for the actress to walk. The camera was in place. It was a dull day and we needed lights to enable filming to take place.

If I asked the assistant film director on the movie when an Italian electrician would be released to light our interview set, I asked him twenty times. Twenty times I got the same reply - *he will be there as soon as we have finished this shot.* I was on edge. Barry Norman had submitted his questions in advance to the star - that was a condition of the interview and something which would not be condoned today - and he seemed relaxed in the railway carriage as he awaited the arrival of Miss Loren. It is the producer who sorts out the logistical problems. When I approached the assistant director for the 21st time, I was informed that the crew had broken for lunch but he assured me that before they resumed filming the movie in the afternoon, they would light my railway compartment so that the interview could take place. Consequently I released the TV crew for their lunch break. I broke the news to the other Barry. He went off too to get some nosh.

Two minutes later a woman approached me and said, *Miss Loren will do the interview now.* I panicked inside but calmly suggested she do it after lunch. *Miss Loren will not be here then. We do it now or not at all,* came the reply from her assistant. I summoned Barry and the crew swiftly back from lunch but the bolshie Italian electrician would not budge and I was powerless to do anything about it.

At that precise moment the sun came out and bathed the railway compartment with light. I ran along the railway platform and grabbed any spare parchment lying there, no longer required by the movie's lighting technicians. I taped it haphazardly to the carriage windows. A diffuse glow emerged as Sophia Loren entered the compartment. Italian screen actresses are almost as conscious of lighting as Italian actors, so her first words were *no lights?* She sat down. I explained that the cameraman was getting a wonderful picture through his viewfinder without them. Phew!

The interview went well and Barry crept in one question which had not been submitted. Being a true professional, the actress replied. When it was over she chided that he was naughty to have done so. But that was all. She left the carriage after I had thanked her profusely and the other Barry had finished flirting with her. The sun went in and the carriage became dull again.

Sophia Loren was one of the most stunning people I have ever seen in my life. She is tall and gracious, voluptuous yet classy. Her high cheekbones offset her almond-shaped green eyes and her gently waved brown hair flows casually from her forehead. She does not wear heavy make-up as her complexion is flawless. I was glad of the opportunity to film her and after the panic of the previous hour, I was immensely relieved. And you know what? The Italian electrician never came near us after his lunch break. I returned to London elated with my coup.

Three days later the phone rang. It was my publicist friend Fred Hift in London. Miss Loren was not pleased that the interview was done without any lighting. She would not permit the interview to be broadcast until she had seen the rushes and approved the technical quality of the film.

This was impossible; the telecast, a few days hence, had been announced in the press. We reached a compromise. If Fred approved the visual quality of the film, it could be transmitted without her seeing it. That afternoon Fred duly turned up at a tiny preview theatre in TV Centre. The lights dimmed, the projectionist ran the film. Sophia Loren looked magnificent.

Eleven   A Kirk in Scotland and a Larry in Dorset

Kirk Douglas came to Scotland in 1971 to make one of his most unmemorable films *Catch Me A Spy* (USA title *To Catch A Spy*). He was available to be interviewed. If you want to interview movie stars, never try to do it in their home town or city. They always refuse, they are too busy living. Like most human beings, when they are away from home and not conducting a discreet affair, they become easily bored. Always try to interview them on location. They have time to spare and egos to be massaged. Invariably they say *yes*. On hearing that Kirk Douglas was filming near the west coast town of Oban I quickly arranged to interview him. Tony Bilbow was unavailable for the trip so I was to be interviewer as well as director. My P.A. Irene came with me and our film crew came from Glasgow.

Early in the day we went down to a loch and watched a ferry leave the quay several times, take after take. It was boring and unexciting and from the shore Kirk was hard to spot on board. But we needed location footage to supplement the interview so film it we did. The Glasgow TV cameraman shot the scene from a couple of angles and that was it. In movies everything has to be perfect before a director can move on to the next scene. Kirk Douglas, being the pro he is, sailed on that car ferry over and over again without complaint. He then disappeared. He did not join the crew at the location lunch site up the road.

One of the joys of filming is the location catering. You just line up outside a converted bus where plenty of high carbohydrate, high cholesterol but delicious food is served. You take it to a nearby table and tuck in. There is not much chatter as everyone is too hungry, having been up since five. The caterers have already provided a full English breakfast on arrival on location, then bacon sandwiches with tea or coffee for the mid-morning break. Now it was one o'clock and time for more comfort food.

That was what it was like making movies in Britain in the 1970s. In those days visitors were welcome to join the crew and partake of whatever was on offer. So as I stood in line for fish and chips and mushy peas, I was astonished to see a very beautiful woman in front of me. As she took her plate of food, she turned and smiled at me. I realised it was Lee Remick, the American actress star of *Anatomy of a Murder* and *Days of Wine and Roses*. The press handout had given me no indication that this comedy thriller featured such a prestigious actress as Miss Remick. Kirk Douglas' co-star was someone I had never heard of, the French actress Marlene Jobert. It was a British/French co-production, that's why.

I was intrigued by Lee Remick and noticed that, during lunch, she sat with the assistant film director, Kip Gowans. I could tell they were in love. I expected glamorous screen actresses to marry handsome screen actors. Sometimes they marry more ordinary but nicer blokes, like Kip. In fact, they were not married then, they both had other partners, but when their respective divorces came through they married and stayed together until her untimely death from cancer in 1991 at the age of 55.

I was informed just after lunch that as Kirk Douglas would not be needed for filming during the next hour or so, he would be available for the promised interview. I had assiduously prepared my questions from the fabulous press cuttings service available at the BBC. I was grateful then for the comprehensive range of stories about this Hollywood actor. I knew he was born in 1916 as Issur Danielovitch Demsky, that he had married twice and had four sons; the eldest, Michael, had just started his own movie career.

Kirk Douglas had his own production company, Bryna Films, named after his mother. He started in theatre and made his first movie at the age of 30, *The Strange Love of Martha Ivers,* a gripping melodrama with Barbara Stanwyck as his leading lady. One of his finest films was *Ace in the Hole,* directed by Billy Wilder, in which Douglas as a ruthless newspaper reporter exploits a human interest story for his own gain. But the film most moviegoers remember him in was *Champion,* where he played an unscrupulous boxer who fought his way to the top. He was 33 when he made it and in it he displayed the muscular body of a much younger athlete. That was because he was fanatical about physical fitness, according to the press cuttings.

In almost every newspaper, he was referred to him as 6'. I am over 5' 10" tall and when I met Kirk Douglas he was no taller. He was 55 years old but people don't shrink two inches in middle age, do they?

To be fair, despite his height Kirk Douglas lived up to expectations. He was relaxed, articulate and informative, particularly about his intensive preparation for the role of the Dutch painter, Vincent van Gogh in *Lust for Life.* He had to learn to hold a paintbrush the correct way and look as if he'd been creating the painter's unique style all his life. He was fortunate that he had the same colouring as the painter so no great make-up sessions were required before each day's filming.

Before I travelled to Scotland for the interview, in order to acquaint myself more fully with Kirk Douglas' film career, I had re-screened this film and Stanley Kubrick's *Paths of Glory* and *Spartacus*. In those days this required an enormous amount of effort. The 35mm or 16mm print had to be located and taken to a projection room of a pre-booked cinema. A projectionist screened the film, changing reels on cue several times during each movie. It was a labour-intensive process and expensive, all of which came off the programme budget. Today's TV producers take for granted how simple it is to screen a movie. You rent or hire it from a local store, take it home and view it in the office, or even online. It is quick and cheap. That's how it should be. I simply state the fact to remind everyone how time consuming it was in those days.

Cinemagoers today probably remember Kirk Douglas as Michael's dad. I enjoyed my time with this Hollywood legend and thought kindly upon him as a worldly yet self-effacing man. As I walked away down the hill to the car to take Irene and me back to Oban, I saw a man sitting under a tree. He murmured to us, *why don't you interview his driver and find out what a real bastard he is?*

The following year I took the film crew to Athelhampton House near Tolpuddle in Dorset, this time with Tony Bilbow in tow. I was director of a location report about the making of the 1972 movie *Sleuth* starring Laurence Olivier and Michael Caine, directed by Joseph L. Mankiewicz. On my arrival I was impressed. The production team had found the ideal country house. The script called for a sequence featuring a large hedge maze and beside this ideal country house stood the ideal maze. I asked the set designer how long it had taken his team to find such a place with such a fantastic maze. *It's all fake*, he replied. I should have known!

The opening sequence was being shot whilst we were there. On a crane about 80 ft high was a new contraption, a Steadicam. I had never seen one before. This was state-of-the-art. It was operated from a video monitor on the ground so the director could see exactly what each shot looked like without having to endanger his well-being by dangling from a crane. All through this long, sweeping sequence the revolutionary camera remained steady. This was 1972. Over 30 years later the use of video cameras and monitors to assist movie-making is commonplace just as they are used daily in hospitals and at railway stations. Nowadays the Steadicam is also used in TV productions. Lower hiring charges have made this possible. This is what excites me. Someone invents a machine for a specific purpose. It then evolves and is used in other areas which the inventor could not possibly have envisaged.

The first interview we filmed was with the director Joseph L. Mankiewicz. I had been apprehensive about meeting such a distinguished film-maker, the man who wrote and directed *All About Eve, The Barefoot Contessa, Suddenly Last Summer* and the oversized and over-budget *Cleopatra,* the epic Taylor and Burton vehicle with a cast of thousands. Now Mankiewicz was using his prodigious talent to direct *Sleuth* with a cast of only two (although for the sake of the plot the opening credits imply there are more). What a perceptive man he turned out to be. I was to visit his home in Connecticut a decade later and although he had had a stroke by then, his insights into Hollywood were accurate and acerbic; he also admitted having an affair with Judy Garland. On location in Dorset he was charming and co-operative, the consummate professional.

The next interview was with the playwright Anthony Shaffer. This was one of those rare occasions when Mankiewicz had not written the screenplay. The Englishman, twin brother of the better known playwright Peter Shaffer, was articulate and pleasant. Then came the usual self deprecating, amusing, delightful interview with Michael Caine - he always did a good turn for the TV cameras. So far we had not caught sight of the great Olivier himself. I think we filmed the producer,

Morton Gottlieb, but interviews with movie producers are unmemorable.

I am going to let you into a trade secret. Whenever TV crews appear on film sets the producers are always on hand. They can hardly wait to be interviewed and as they are funding the whole shebang, we usually oblige with a swift chat. More often than not, everything they say ends up on the cutting room floor. In those days, film stock and processing were expensive items on the programme budget. So I had an arrangement with the cameraman that, just before the interview began, he would say, *do you want a French filter on this one, Barry?* The producer would be flattered because although he had limited technical knowledge, he was aware that filters on camera lens enhanced the finished image. Invariably I would respond with, *yes please.* This was the signal that the cameraman would film the interview without any film in the camera. It saved us a fortune.

We did not know when Olivier was going to appear so we had a break behind another part of the fake hedge, well out of the sight lines of the movie crew. Suddenly we were aware of a mellifluous voice reciting the names of flowers plus a brief description of where to plant them and how to tend them. The voice was too distinctive to be the head gardener at this country house and the man was too knowledgeable to be the lord of the manor. I peeped around the corner. It was a most endearing sight. Olivier was giving his co-star a lesson in gardening. If he had not been tempted by Hollywood in later life and appearing in such appalling movies as *The Betsy* and a remake of *The Jazz Singer*, he could have been a worthy TV presenter of *Gardeners' World*.

Michael Caine, born Maurice Micklewhite in the East End of London, was now a man of property including a residence by the Thames. He was nearly 40, an age when a man's thoughts turn to roses, begonias and hydrangeas. He had the perfect mentor. You could tell the two actors had a great rapport despite their different backgrounds. It was just as well, they were the only two in the film. They had no other colleagues to moan about.

Before we filmed the Olivier interview, we wanted to capture on celluloid the rehearsal of a scene before the movie's 'take'. We could never start rolling a 16mm camera for TV when the 35mm camera was shooting a scene because of unwanted camera noise. Consequently most TV cameramen know how to be discreet on a movie set. They do not obstruct the gigantic apparatus entailed in the movie-making process. By standing surreptitiously at the side of the set or from a staircase looking down, they can get some fantastic shots without the movie director or actors noticing.

Not Olivier. He knew that he sometimes fluffed lines on a 'take' and nearly always did so at rehearsal. He did not wish to tarnish his illustrious image by having TV cameras record this phenomenon. He spoke quietly to the assistant director and we were forbidden to shoot. You could not blame him .The formal interview which followed was precisely that, a formal interview. Olivier acted it, the way he acted that dreadful, incomprehensible acceptance speech when he received an honorary Oscar towards the end of his life.

The good thing about *Sleuth* was that Laurence Olivier, Michael Caine and Jospeh L. Mankiewicz all received Academy Award nominations. And these days whenever I see a maze, I touch it to see if it's real.

Twelve

In the Cannes & Elsewhere

I have only been to the Cannes Film Festival twice in my life - in 1973 and 1975 and I never want to go again. To me it was a nightmare. Perhaps it is more congenial when you do not have the pressure of making a TV documentary about the event, which has to be edited and transmitted by the end of the Festival.

It was Michael Caine who explained the importance of the Festival in an interview I filmed with him there. *It is not the films that matter, it's the people you meet. In one week in Cannes you can have meaningful discussions with Hollywood and international producers and directors that would otherwise take ten months of travelling.* Not a lot of people know that!

When you arrive in Cannes and have checked in to a dingy hotel several blocks back from the fashionable Croisette on the sea front - all the major hotels are booked out months in advance at inflated prices - the first thing you have to do is register as a Member of the Press in order to get access to certain buildings and events. It's called *accreditation*. I was bemused by the French bureaucracy at the Palais des Festivals, an attractive, purpose built edifice near the famous Carlton Hotel and now superseded by a concrete monstrosity down by the marina, nicknamed *The Bunker.*

I waited in line with many others seeking accreditation. The queue became longer and longer as an attractive and impeccably manicured blonde French woman spoke languidly on the phone from a nearby desk, eyeing each of us as she spoke. After several minutes, she hung up. *Service at last,* I thought. It was not to be. Staring straight at us, the blonde moved to another phone, dialled a number and spoke for several more minutes. Eventually she deigned to come to the counter where she insisted on speaking only in French. Her arrogance was outlandish.

Where do you start to make a programme when the world and his dog are there? Those you want to interview are hidden away at the fabulously expensive Hotel du Cap at Antibes, several miles along the coast. The camera crew get their atmospheric shots - the palm-lined promenade, the Carlton, Majestic and Martinque Hotels all emblazoned with giant movie posters; they film people walking up the steps of the Palais des Festivals; or a starlet or two on the beach baring almost all for the world's paparazzi; plus shots of other film crews who seem to be making a better fist of things than you.

Traffic moves at a snail's pace as stretch limousines wend their way along the Croisette. Local youths on noisy motor scooters dodge precariously in and out of this melange of expensive cars. Elderly widows with freshly coiffured pink hair stroll by with their tiny and equally well-groomed poodles, stopping at each elegant lamp post along the way, going nowhere in particular. Men in berets with faces grizzled by the sun walk bow-legged with a Gitane hanging from their lips.

Visitors crowd the promenade. But the best shots are those of tie-less, gold-chained movie producers with large cigars and a gaggle of girls, sitting on the Carlton Terrace paying exorbitant prices for bourbon on the rocks, espresso coffee or citron pressé. This is where the deals are done. Occasionally a star or director joins the exclusive throng but generally this is producer territory.

While the cameraman and sound recordist have been doing their best to capture some 'atmosphere', my P.A. Irene and I spend every precious moment trying to pin down interviews with stars and directors. Mayhem reigns. Every film publicist looks frazzled as the media tries to milk every ounce of column inches or TV exposure from their stable of stars, most of whom have come to languish in luxurious hotel suites overlooking the Mediterranean, enjoy superb French cuisine, fine wines and a good lay, in return for as little public exposure as possible.

After grabbing a few minutes on camera down on the Carlton pier with the then little known and asthmatic director Martin Scorsese who had just made *Mean Streets,* I had to dash up to the temporary Paramount Pictures office to collect Donald Sutherland and escort him down to join Tony Bilbow and the film crew for our second interview of the day. Whilst running up the office stairs, I noticed a man wearing a hat and sunglasses running down the stairs. He nodded as he passed and I continued my journey. When I reached the office, I was told that Donald Sutherland had just left. Of course! It was the actor himself who had acknowledged me on the stairs. I was too keyed up to recognise him. We never got that interview. Cannes is like that. And the last thing a TV director can do is find the time to see a movie. In my two visits there I saw a total of four films, one of them purely for pleasure, *Gloria* directed by John Cassevetes and starring his wife Gena Rowlands. The screening started at midnight and, despite a heavy day of filming, I did not doze through one frame of it.

I remember filming a very good interview with Richard Benjamin, who had starred in *The Last of Sheila.* He was confident enough as a human being to share his doubts and vulnerability with a TV audience. I enjoyed meeting the director Joseph Losey because he had directed my favourite film *Accident*. I asked him how he had managed to shoot a night scene which ended with a shot of a huge jet flying overhead - the cameraman instinctively panned up to it, unplanned but perfect.

I decided to film the actress Geraldine Chaplin, Charlie's daughter, beside a pretty fountain at the Majestic Hotel where she was staying. She had a rather soft, beguiling voice to match her delicate features but could barely be heard over the tinkling of the fountain. There was no time to move elsewhere. It was hell trying to edit it back in London - water from a fountain is surprisingly inconsistent.

Dustin Hoffman was in town too. It coincided with the European premiere of *Lenny*, a biography of the troubled American nightclub comic Lenny Bruce He gave a press conference with his co-star Valerie Perrine which we were allowed to film but were not granted an interview with the star. At the Majestic Hotel, not far from where I had filmed Miss Chaplin, I saw an Austrian film crew setting up their equipment. Then Dustin Hoffman arrived to be interviewed. I was furious with the movie's distributors for snubbing our request, so got my cameraman to hide behind a hedge and film Dustin Hoffman being interviewed by others. Sometimes a man's gotta do what a man's gotta do.

A gentleman accosted me at the Carlton Hotel. This is where people lie in wait to meet those they need to see. Eventually everyone enters the foyer of this sea-front hotel at some time during the Festival, so if you have the patience you can chat to almost anyone. Dr. Harry Urban told me that his 14 year old son, Stuart, was the youngest person ever to have a film shown at Cannes. As the boy came from Kingston, Surrey this was news. I agreed to view his offspring's 14 minute offering *The Virus of War* and film an interview with the lad the following day. I can no longer remember the storyline but it was competently directed by Stuart using young actors, including his 12 year old brother Mark. I suspect that a professional adult or two had helped with the editing but I conveniently forgot that.

I discussed with Harry a suitable location for the filming of the interview. He suggested we all meet at his hotel for lunch and film the interview immediately afterwards. *Which hotel?* I enquired. *Hotel Du Cap*, was his reply. Irene and I did a double-take. This was the favourite haunt of visiting Hollywood stars. Dr Urban must be terribly rich or incredibly ostentatious. All I can say is that he was an extraordinarily generous host, his wife, Josephine, was a darling and the boys were polite and somewhat overawed at the prospect of an interview for BBC2. We filmed both brothers on the rocks at the front of this luxurious hotel right on the Mediterranean. The setting was memorable and Stuart gave a polished performance for a 14 year old. We did not need to interview Mark really, but we had been treated to a good lunch so why not? Back in London, Mark's contribution ended up on the cutting room floor. That experience had a great impact on him. When he grew up he became an intrepid reporter for BBC2's flagship current affairs programme *Newsnight* and an author of several books on military history. He is an excellent communicator. Stuart, too, went from strength to strength as a TV drama and later movie director, winning a Best TV Drama BAFTA Award for his BBC film about the Falkland's War *A Gentleman's Agreement*. He also wrote and directed the less prestigious movie *Preaching to the Perverted*. It has been fascinating to watch the brothers grow into talented and responsible men with loving families of their own. And it all started on the French Riviera.

I was excited when the President of the Jury of the Cannes Film Festival agreed to be interviewed for *Film Night* right at the end of our stay. She would comment on the quality of films the jury had seen in competition and how their final decision would be reached. It was a perfect climax to our TV report. I was even more excited when I met The President, for it was Ingrid Bergman. It was not the right time to tell her how I had fallen in love with her in *Notorious* when she drank champagne with Cary Grant in a most erotic love scene. She looked stunningly beautiful in that movie and seemed so sophisticated, a quality in women I have always admired. She still looked good at the age of 57.

The BBC cameraman had set up the camera and lighting ready for her arrival. She knew about movie making and as soon she saw the camera position, she calmly said *higher, higher.* She knew that looking down on a middle aged woman's face was far more flattering - it did not reveal an ageing neck. A learned another lesson in film-making.

When I returned to the Cannes Film Festival two years later, I visited Hotel du Cap again, to a buffet lunch hosted by Sir Lew Grade, now venturing from TV into movies. The green and white decor of the sea-front dining area was simple elegance at its best. After helping myself to a superb array of French cuisine - fresh lobster with avocado, salade nicoise, wild strawberries with fromage frais - I sat patiently as Sir Lew abandoned his long cigar to announce his cluster of movie projects. There is only one title I remember. Imagine a man called Les; then imagine someone being miserable. That is how the tycoon pronounced his forthcoming remake of the Victor Hugo classic, *Les Miserables.* But it was a great lunch.

Every evening the crowds gathered outside the Palais des Festivals, just down the road from the Carlton Hotel. Occasionally the actors would walk there but usually they travelled in stretch limousines. The excitement of the crowd as each star arrived and the applause they received would have warmed the cockles of even Scrooge's heart. It would reach a crescendo as they moved up the red carpeted steps and into the building for the screening of the gala movie. It was like Oscar night by the sea. Evening wear was compulsory and I assume every well known designer was represented, so glamorous were the outfits.

Amidst the screams of the crowds came the flashing bulbs of the world's press. I needed to capture the excitement of such an event at least once for my documentary. As the assigned cameraman was not a movie buff, I stood next to him to ensure he filmed the star and not the ubiquitous producer's wife or mistress. It was an experience I shall never forget. Everyone *had* to get a good picture and every cameraman used the strength of a Rugby footballer to achieve it. I was pushed and pummelled and I pummelled and pushed with the determination and ferocity I could muster. At the same time the crushing sensation of a stampede was ever present. The sequence looked great on TV. Everything seemed so civilised.

I had a hectic time trying to capture the spirit of the Festival for British viewers. Late each evening I would return exhausted to my unfashionable hotel, ready to collapse into bed. Unfortunately the night concierge had seen my Australian passport on arrival and as he had spent several years in Sydney, my home town, he wanted to reminisce with me as he kept a lonely vigil. He achieved this by reciting to me on my weary return the names of Sydney suburbs, *Maroubra, Cronulla, Kogarah, Wahroonga, Parramatta.* It was the last thing I wanted to hear but every evening he continued the litany *Turramurra, Hurstville, Dee Why, Coogee, Killara..* He smiled somewhat nostalgically as he pronounced each extraordinary word. As I wrested myself away from his relentless wittering, I could only manage to undress, clean my teeth and hop into bed. Washing my underwear was not a priority.

After my flight back from Nice to London, I was standing at the carousel at Heathrow's Terminal 2 waiting for my suitcase filled with dirty laundry to come bouncing down the chute. Also waiting were actors Roger Moore and Hywel Bennett and singer Vera Lynn, none of whom I had spotted at Cannes. I was so embarrassed when my case arrived. The latch had broken and my unclean underpants and sweat-stained shirts preceded the case itself. In front of these luminaries, I raced around grabbing the offending garments and took my damaged bag to the Air France desk hoping for compensation. Instead they gave me the address of a repair shop in distant south London, miles away from my north London home. The airline would only bear the cost of the repair. Instead I threw the suitcase away, bought a new one and did not travel with Air France for another 15 years. Serves them right.

Once back in London, the marathon began. The programme was to be transmitted on the last night of the Festival, just after the results of the Films in Competition had been announced. I had filmed a wide shot of Cannes at night which ran for two minutes. This would end the programme, over which the names of the winners would be announced. I thought this would be an ingenious way of making the programme more relevant and topical.

Once all the 16mm film from the trip had been processed and the ¼" audio tapes had been transferred to 16mm magnetic tape and synchronised to the picture, I was able to start work in the cutting room with my film editor. This would be my home for 36 hours non-stop. I had little time to be contemplative about my 'work of art'. I had to decide quickly how the programme would begin, then what would follow and in which order.

While I was being oh so decisive and suggesting to my editor which shots should be used, the other side of my brain was telling me an alternative scenario. It was a weird feeling which I had to ignore. I only had time to follow my initial instinct. The BBC is a wonderful place to work late at night. Snack food, tea and coffee are available and how welcome they are when everything else is quiet around you, save for the scene shifters who are dissembling unused sets from the studios and assembling new ones for another show the next morning. There are shaving and shower facilities too, but I was too busy to contemplate that. The edited documentary was ready on time, the commentary was added and the rest of the soundtrack dubbed, thus smoothing over the rough edges.

Hundreds of movies from all over the world are screened at Cannes, both in an out of competition and in the marketplace which is an ancillary part of the Festival. I was proud of the movies I had been able to cover in this *Film Night Special*. Transmission time arrived. The programme began and my documentary looked good and several pertinent film clips from movies in the festival were shown.

The last shot appeared, we crossed 'live' to a telephone report announcing which film had won the Palme D'Or. It was a dark horse, a Greek film few thought had a chance. Its title had not even been mentioned once in the preceding 35 minute documentary. You can't win 'em all.

In 1975 I was invited to be President of the Jury at the Cork Short Film Festival. I flew to Cork shortly after my last Cannes trip. The contrast could not have been greater. Compared to the Mediterranean town, Cork is not stunning, but it's OK. The food is good, plain Irish cooking with not a hint of garlic. The hotels were not luxurious and overpriced but comfortable and faded. As for the people, Cork wins hands down. They are friendly, cheerful and positive.

On the down side, three women journalists I chatted to during my ten days there all told me their fathers had died of alcoholism. Perhaps it is too taxing to be friendly, cheerful and positive all the time. In Cannes I was treated like dirt, in Cork like a king.

The Irish army had been seconded to look after jury members, so whenever I stepped out of my hotel, a car was waiting to drive me anywhere I wished. On the night of my arrival, I decided I would go for a walk around the town so released the driver. Although I had never visited the city before, I felt comfortable and at ease. Perhaps I had been a leprechaun in a past life. Everything seemed familiar, especially its people. Then it dawned on me. The inhabitants of Cork looked like Australians. Irish immigration Down Under had been so profuse in previous generations that there was the answer. Even the roast dinners at the hotel, a daily occurrence, tasted like Australian baked dinners. The only difference I noticed were the serving of both roast and boiled potatoes with every meal. Since the previous century's famine, the Irish were never going to be short of potatoes again.

I shall never forget my meeting the next morning with my fellow jurors. An Irish author and film historian, Liam O'Leary, suggested a scoring system. He had been on many juries and it had worked well. As we had over 70 short films to view, I was willing to listen. His logic was so Irish I have to recount it.

If a fillum is very good with a chance of winning the top prize, give it one point. If a fillum is good and could have a chance of winning the top prize - if there aren't any really good ones - give it two points. If a fillum is average with no chance of winning anything, give it three points. But if a fillum is really terrible give it no points at all…zero.

When I told him for reasons of logic that I would give a bad film four points, he could not fathom such an absurd statement. The Irish are a law unto themselves.

Although we spent each day viewing short films for the prize-giving at the end of the Festival, each evening would be spent watching premieres of recent feature films, mostly American. Sure enough, the army car would be waiting outside the hotel and I would be driven to the cinema. I stepped from the car onto the red carpet from the pavement to the foyer. Crowds lined the pavement to get a good look - at whom? The only famous movie person I saw during the whole Festival was Jane Seymour and this was long before she became TV's *Dr. Quinn, Medicine Woman.*

The only other notable face was that of a former Irish Prime Minister, Charles Haughey who was a Cork man. As I strode from the car to each screening, I *felt* like a star, wholly oblivious to the obvious disappointment of the crowd who did not recognise me from Adam. I was interviewed by the Press and on local radio. I was certainly bobbing around Cork. I even kissed the Blarney Stone on a drive out of town to the famous castle.

Even though my scoring system was at variance with the Irish jury member, my team and I had viewed our final film ahead of schedule. I suggested everyone write down on separate pieces of paper their 1st, 2nd and 3rd choices in each category. I would check them and then we would all discuss the differences to produce a final list. Each list was remarkably similar. Good films emerge of their own accord. I chaired a brief debate with my colleagues and in no time at all we had chosen the winners in all categories. It was only at the presentation ceremony that I realised that the winning list was my original list. Until then I had been unaware that I was a control freak. I learned a lot in Ireland.

The London Film Festival is less exciting because it prides itself on offering no prizes - it shows the best from the world's other film festivals. I was duty bound to attend, particularly on opening night, a black tie affair with a great party afterwards. Each year the theme of the party was built around the country of origin of the chosen opening film. This was fine when it was an Indian or Japanese movie. The decor was elaborate and the food appropriate and usually delicious.

All changed the year a Dutch movie was chosen. I cannot remember its title but the opening night party featured international, rather than Dutch cuisine. After the screening I was spotted leaving the National Film Theatre auditorium by the then BBC Managing Director, Huw Wheldon. His wife had been unable or unwilling to attend, he did not say, so he was alone. He was pleased to see me and en route to the party, put his arm around me as we left the auditorium and chatted about the merits of the chosen movie. I thought to myself *I have manipulated this situation entirely.* This is how it came about.

When I was a humble producer, whenever I got into the lift at TV Centre and Wheldon got in too, I always nodded to him and smiled. He gave me a quizzical look which suggested *should I know you?* After eighteen more months of my nodding and smiling, his look changed. He must have thought, *yes I do know you, even though I do not know your name.* Six months later we encountered each other at the festival. I was his best pal that evening. That's how things work in television. Who you know and who you are seen with are important.

The Edinburgh Film Festival, held to coincide with the main Arts Festival each August, was a more esoteric affair. Its director in the early 1970s was Lynda Myles who went on to become a successful TV and movie producer. As Festival Director she needed TV coverage and *Film Night* was the only programme she could approach - ITV's *Cinema* was more down-market in her eyes. She came to London well in advance to announce her plans. I was stunned. Here was I, producer of a weekly TV film programme, yet I did not recognise one title she mentioned. I later realised she was using movie-speak.

When she announced they would be presenting the UK premiere of, say, *Encounters,* it did not dawn on me immediately that she meant *Close Encounters of the Third Kind.* You get the drift. I became quite depressed when she then said that there would be a Herzog retrospective. Who was he or she for that matter - an ageing movie star, an obscure German cameraman, a deceased production designer? You never knew with Edinburgh. Remember, this was before Werner Herzog had directed *Aguirre Wrath of God, The Enigma of Kaspar Hauser, Nosferatu* or *Fitzcarraldo.* I could not enquire whether or not he would be attending the Festival, he (or she) might have been dead ten years for all I knew.

She then let slip that Sam Fuller (a director whose work I knew) would also be there with Werner. This implied that a man called Herzog was in the land of the living and might be a director, because Sam Fuller had directed such American classics as *I Shot Jesse James, Hell and High Water* and *Run of the Arrow.* Yes, Edinburgh also indulged the cult of the 'B' movie. I enjoyed every trip to the Edinburgh Film Festival. It might have been an eclectic choice of movies but it was always stimulating.

On one visit I met and chatted to the American director Brian De Palma. He had made a film called *Obsession* and was about to make *Carrie.* His best known, *Dressed to Kill,* was yet to come. He was completely unaware of the resurgence of Australian cinema - he had never heard of *Picnic at Hanging Rock.* I persuaded him to sit through a new Australian movie that was about to be screened called *Mad Dog Morgan.* Although there was a local cast, the legendary Australian outlaw of the title was played by the American actor Dennis Hopper of *Easy Rider* fame. I could not have chosen a more violent or unrepresentative Aussie film if I had tried. It was even too violent for Brian De Palma.

There was a relaxing Members Area by the main Festival cinema. There you could grab a beer and a sandwich between screenings and catch up on the plethora of publicity material which had been stuffed into your allocated press box. One afternoon I collected my coffee and bun and sat beside a big bear of a man with a shock of thick blond hair. He held out his hand and said, *hi, I'm Nick Nolte.* It was that kind of town.

I actually attended one of the few Manila Film Festivals held in the early 1980s, before President Marcos and his wife Imelda were deposed. So courtesy Philippine Airways, every man and his mistress were flown there and allocated accommodation in a leading hotel. Mine was the Manila Hotel itself, a palace of a place with a guard on every floor. A special Festival Center had been built by the Marcos', using taxpayers' money, not from their private Swiss bank accounts. The Center was all concrete and ostentation, like many of the surrounding buildings. The Marcos regime certainly put their mark on Manila. It was completed just in time for the opening, hastened by the fact that when eight local Filipinos fell to their deaths during construction, they poured the concrete over them to save time. That was the rumour doing the rounds by the time I arrived.

I had a local TV film crew placed at my disposal - an easy task for the Marcos regime to arrange. From my observation, there was one TV channel allocated to cover every official function the President and his First Lady attended, halting other programmes immediately in order to cross 'live' to a particular event.

There were plenty of stars and directors for me to film. Jeremy Irons was there for the Asian premiere of *The French Lieutenant's Woman,* Peter Ustinov was promoting his role as Hercule Poirot in *Evil Under the Sun,* as was the film's director, Guy Hamilton. Lord Lew Grade was depressed because the failure of *Raise the Titanic* had brought his ITC movie company to its knees, but he was in Manila to attend the premiere of his more successful venture *On Golden Pond.* The noted Indian director, Satyajit Ray was happy that his latest offering was being screened; the American director John Frankenheimer was promoting *The Challenge.* I interviewed them all.

One day whilst waiting for an interviewee to arrive, I saw a strange-looking woman approach the swimming area. She wore a high-cut bikini. Had she been a few inches shorter, I'd have mistaken her for a dwarf. A phalanx of photographers appeared from nowhere and I watched this obviously pre-arranged photo-call with astonishment. She was the epitome of exhibitionism. I asked a journalist who she was and was told it was Pia Zadora. She had married a very rich older man who had financed her films. Her latest, *Butterfly,* was to be screened that evening. I saw another movie instead.

I went to several lavish parties, including one attended by President Marcos and Imelda. She carried on the Filipino tradition of wearing, at all social events, long dresses with high, straight, sleeves which stood erect from the shoulders. She had instructed her socialite hangers-on to wear the same style. He wore a white uniform with lots of braid. Later in the evening something strange happened. Imelda Marcos sang. Her voice was OK and she obviously enjoyed performing but it is something you do not expect from a First Lady.

I shall never forget the last night of the Festival where awards were handed out and other accolades acknowledged. It was held at the Festival Center. I cannot recall which film was shown, but afterwards, President Marcos, who surprised me by being quite charming, gave a rambling speech and then invited us to attend the Farewell Banquet at a nearby building. The local Filipinos who had lined the streets, held Imelda Marcos in high esteem - there was no doubt about that, even though she owned more pairs of shoes than they had had hot dinners.

The TV station covered the whole proceedings on their State-owned channel. The guests, including myself, wandered slowly to the banquet hall and waited, and waited and waited. Apparently Mrs. Marcos had returned to the Palace to change her outfit. It must have taken her ages to find matching shoes because she was gone a very long time. What the TV station transmitted in the interim was anybody's guess, but in due course we were aware of her arrival with the President. TV coverage was back on track. It was 10.45pm and no food could be served to guests until they had arrived. I was starving. Drums started rolling, a military band played in quick-march tempo and the Marcos' made their grand entrance. It was reminiscent of Mussolini in Fascist Italy. It was frightening.

Before the meal was served, several prizes had to be awarded. The trophies were tall, elegant, well designed pieces of bronze sculpture. I was impressed. The Indian actor/ producer, Shashi Kapoor was given one for his performance in Merchant-Ivory's *Heat and Dust*. After the prize-giving and still no food, there was another drum roll. Two young Filipino men marched, carrying a velvet cushion on which was placed the Filipino version of legion d'honneur. Behind them, wearing a white tunic and marching purposefully was the London film critic Alexander Walker. He acknowledged his award with great solemnity, his chest filled with pride. It was farcical.

As the awards continued and our stomachs rumbled even more, we lost interest at our table and, like many others nearby, started to chat. The gentle applause continued as more and more accolades were acknowledged. Suddenly I heard the words *BBC* and *Barry Brown*. I got up from my distant table and nodded my acceptance of whatever had been said while those around me applauded. To do this day I have no idea why I was singled out for praise.

About 18 months later I flew to Bombay (now Mumbai) to cover a movie Shashi Kapoor was making. I visited a typical Indian bungalow, the official headquarters of his production company. On the veranda stood the Best Actor statuette he had received at the Manila Film Festival. It had rusted badly. It was made of tin, not bronze. It was typical of the Marcos regime, all glitter and little substance. Not long after, Ferdinand and Imelda were deposed. There has never been another Manila Film Festival.

Thirteen   Pinewood,
Shepperton & Elstree

If I tell you I never want to visit a movie studio again as
long as I live, you would not believe me. It is something
many moviegoers dream of. It is sometimes offered as a
prize in a magazine or newspaper competition. The hours
and hours I have stood on hard concrete floors or shivered
uncontrollably on the back lot waiting for something to
happen, would equal the time spent at the World Chess
Championships. The motto on movie and TV locations is
"hurry up and wait" - the bigger the studio, the longer the
wait.

Pinewood, the largest UK studio is in Iver, Buckinghamshire;
Shepperton is down by the river Thames in Middlesex
and Elstree and the nearby Borehamwood studios are in
Hertfordshire. Whenever *Film Night* was invited on to a
movie set with a BBC film crew, it meant an early start
from London. On arrival I usually met the allocated 16mm
crew for the first time and we all had to be members of the
Cinema and TV trade union to be allowed in.

A TV film cameraman has to have a patient and compassionate disposition to be successful on a movie set. He has to be tactful and deferential to the needs of the movie. Very few BBC cameramen had those qualities. Most were too 'bolshie' to adapt to these circumstances. There were a few who fitted the bill admirably and I requested them whenever I could. It made life so much easier.

At first it was so exciting to be able to visit these famous studios, whose names I had recognised from the closing credits of movies I had seen in Australia a generation earlier. But one's patience wears thin when the film publicist, who has made all the arrangements, cannot deliver what he or she has promised. To be fair, they cannot prejudge the preoccupation, mood swings or whims of their stars, but sometimes I wondered whether they had even let anyone know we were coming until we arrived.

The ideal situation is this. On arrival at the studio, someone greets you, explains what is about to happen on the set, introduces you to the director and assistant director, suggests the best times to interview the stars, takes you to lunch during the studio break, in fact, helps you achieve all you need to in order to make a nicely edited item for your TV programme.

What happened more often than not was this. The publicist arrives later than you, goes straight to the office, leaving you to manage as best you can. I soon learned which publicists to trust and accepted only their invitations. However, if there was a star you were anxious to interview and the publicist on that particular movie was arrogant and inefficient, you persevered. I often had to remind myself of the phrase I had learned years earlier from a psychiatrist - *efficiency is not a human quality.*

I used to think that every movie director was a genius. He *had* to be in order to be in control on the set and also be aware of time and the budget. He had to cope with famous actors,

Barry Brown

be extremely knowledgeable about every technical aspect of movie-making. Wrong. After several years of watching movie directors in action, I believe I could have done as well as many of them. If you believe in yourself, others will. It is an old cliché but true. In retrospect, I realise I preferred the faster pace of TV production and the excitement of transmission deadlines. Movie people seem to have all the time in the world to attain the perfection they crave. They would be the first to disagree, saying that compromise is necessary, just as it is in TV production. Film directors face deadlines too.

In preparing for one edition of *Film Night* I was surprised to notice that the running time for the UK movie release of the big Lerner and Loew musical *Camelot* was 12 minutes shorter than the USA version. I took umbrage. What right did distributors have to edit scenes from a movie to suit their screening schedules? I phoned the USA to contact the film's director Joshua Logan. Was he aware of this shorter version? Of course he was. He told me that he had known the premiere date for the movie at New York's Radio City Music Hall before he had shot one frame of film. He had terrible production problems during the shoot, which gave him less time in the cutting room to meet his deadline. Consequently, he could not fine-tune the editing. For the later international release dates he was able to make it the movie *he* wanted it to be - by making it 12 minutes shorter. So film distributors were not always the monsters I thought they were.

All in all, I filmed TV items about three musicals which were made at Pinewood. Those directors must have had no premiere deadline. The hanging around was interminable. Over and over again I hurried to the studio to be present at the start of the day's filming, then waited hours for anything to happen. The actors were placed strategically on set; the choreographers ensured that the director's planned camera movements did not affect their routines; the playback machine of the pre-recorded songs was set at the level to which the performers could mime.

The first musical I saw being filmed was the *Speakeasy* number for Alan Parker's 1976 film *Bugsy Malone*. It is a gangster movie played by children with splurge guns instead of real weapons. The set looked great and the kids were wonderful in their smart 1920s suits and flapper dresses. Playing Tallulah was 13 year old Jodie Foster. She performed much better than all the other children on the set that day. She was a real pro, bright as a button, quick on the uptake and aware of everything going on around her. I knew she was destined for stardom. Scott Baio, who played Bugsy, was a year older and competent but you knew then he would not flourish as an adult actor. He did a few TV series as a young man then faded from the scene. I hope he stashed his money away.

As I left the *Bugsy Malone* speakeasy set I walked along the 1920s New York street built at Pinewood for the movie, not on the back lot but inside a huge sound stage. It was fabulous and designed and built by British craftsmen. They are the best. On a nearby stage another musical was being shot *The Slipper and the Rose* with Gemma Craven as Cinderella and Richard Chamberlain as Prince Charming.

The ballroom set was all grandeur and chandeliers. The painted patterned floor was perfect for the two of them to waltz together and fall in love before midnight. Richard Chamberlain, as always, gave a charming, if bland interview. He was one of the best looking actors on screen in the mid 1970s. He was tall and lithe with huge brown eyes and a deep voice. He had been TV's *Dr. Kildare* and for the past ten years had established himself as an international film actor playing Tschaikovsky in *The Music Lovers*, Byron in *Lady Caroline Lamb* and Aramis in the umpteenth remake of *The Three Musketeers*. He was the ideal romantic lead and even at 40 he was the perfect Prince Charming.

Some months later when I attended the Press Show of the
film, I was intrigued to see that the orchestral music score
had been conducted by Angela Morley. It was the first
time in years of watching screen credits that I had seen a
woman's name as orchestral conductor. I made enquiries.
Angela Morley was the new name for the well known light-
music composer and conductor Wally Stott. In middle-age,
married with children and grandchildren, he had decided
to become a woman.

The third musical I saw shot at Pinewood was *Mister Quilp*
an adaptation of Dickens' *The Old Curiosity Shop* with
Anthony Newley in the title role. It was being produced
and financed by Readers' Digest during the company's brief
foray into movie making. The producer was Helen Strauss,
a tough but fair New Yorker, well past her sell-by date at the
magazine, I suspect. She had a Rolls Royce at her disposal
during her stay in this country and would be driven the 100
yards from her office to the studio whenever she wished to
visit the set. The financial extravagance of movie budgets
has always appalled me.

The day we visited was the day of Mister Quilp's demise. He
falls into the river and drowns. The water tank at Pinewood
had been filled and a couple of divers were standing by,
as was Mr. Newley's 'double', for the final drop. I was
disappointed. I had travelled many miles out of town with
a BBC film crew and apart from an interview with the star,
all footage I would get for *Film Night* would be a close-up
shot of the star hanging on for dear life, then a wide shot
of the 'double' falling into the water. *Don't worry*, said the
assistant director *there is no way Anthony Newley is going
to use a 'double' when the BBC is filming him.* Sure enough,
the 'double' received his fee for no work that day. Being
the 'ham' that he was, the leading actor spoke his lines
tragically at the edge of the studio tank, then lost his grip
and dropped twenty feet into the murky water. When the
director called *cut*, a soaked Anthony Newley emerged

triumphant. I like egomaniacs. They always do the right thing for the camera.

I only filmed a location report on one musical at Shepperton Studios. It was *Alice's Adventures In Wonderland* in 1972 with a teenage Fiona Fullerton, full of puppy fat, playing Alice. Everyone spoiled her and she was obnoxious. These days she is slim, glamorous, successful and much more amenable. Perhaps we were all like that as teenagers.

It was not a successful movie but no one contemplated that while it was being shot. It had a glittering cast and we were there to film the Mad Hatter's tea party. Michael Crawford was the White Rabbit, Dudley Moore was Dormouse and Peter Sellers the March Hare. Peter Sellers objected to being filmed as an animal and instructed us not to film him in that scene. No matter, we had already filmed the more co-operative Michael Crawford, another egotist. He had let us film him earlier in the day enduring the long make-up and costume process for his role as a rabbit That experience must have come in handy years later for the daunting task of playing the disfigured *Phantom of the Opera* in the Andrew Lloyd Webber musical.

Later that day, I got a chance to chat with the cinematographer, Geoffrey Unsworth. He had just won an Oscar for *Cabaret* and I wanted to ask him how he had achieved that memorable opening shot in the film. In the background you hear the musicians tuning up while you see distorted faces of people at Berlin's sleazy Kit Kat Club. How did he create such a wonderful effect? How did he achieve such distortion? I thought he had used some new-fangled device. Not a bit. He simply crumpled some tin foil and pasted it on the opposite wall. He then pointed the camera at the foil and hey presto, weird and wonderful faces appeared which set the mood for the whole movie.

A teenage Fiona Fullerton was no match, I thought, for Tatum O'Neal whom I filmed at Pinewood a few years later when she was starring in *International Velvet,* the long overdue sequel to *National Velvet* which had made Elizabeth Taylor a star. Five years earlier Tatum had won a Best Supporting Actress Oscar when she made her scene-stealing film debut in *Paper Moon* opposite her father Ryan O'Neal. Her father did not even attend the Oscar ceremony that year because he was miffed that he had not been nominated. Tatum's precocious habits in real life, not helped by her selfish, undisciplined father, had been well documented by the press. I was ready for the monster. It would be a coup to get a filmed interview with her so I was prepared to wait. She was a notoriously bad timekeeper, I had been warned.

I was told she would be ready at 4pm when she had finished her one but last scene for the day. I alerted my crew about the probable delay. Then on the dot of four a pretty 15 year old Tatum O'Neal came over to us with the film's publicist. She was courteous, polite, quiet and rather shy. Was this the abrasive rebel I had been led to expect? She answered each question I put to her calmly but nervously. She made *me* nervous, she was so vulnerable. There was no sign of a wild child. Later in life she married John McEnroe by whom she had three children. He had a wild reputation too and a vicious temper, on the tennis court at least. I knew the marriage would not last. Tatum was too nice to put up with that – but then her wild side returned.

Many of the James Bond films were made at Pinewood. They had even built an additional and enormous water tank in order to film a spectacular submarine sequence in *For Your Eyes Only.* It was most impressive, but the Bond experience I remember best was during the making of *Diamonds Are Forever,* Sean Connery's final film as 007. My P.A Irene was ecstatic at the prospect of meeting this hunk of a sex symbol. We arrived at the studios early and were allocated a dowdy dressing room to set up camera, sound and lights for the interview. By 10am we were ready and waiting for the moment when, between scenes, the Scots-born star would find the time to grant us the promised interview. I was reluctant to release the cameraman to capture any of the usual footage on the set itself, in case he was not around when the star was ready to be interviewed.

Tony Bilbow, having stayed up late the night before to prepare his questions, was getting tired of sitting there waiting hour upon hour. The crew talked amongst themselves at length about all manner of technical problems, BBC bureaucracy and media gossip. I was constantly on the prowl trying to get an indication that the star was on his way. Irene was reluctant to go to the bathroom attached to the dressing room in case Sean Connery arrived whilst she was there. After several hours she could wait no longer.

Then, while she was attending to the call of nature, what she had most feared happened. The star arrived. I can still see the look on her face as she unceremoniously opened the door of the lavatory, only to see her idol, Sean Connery standing opposite her. He was dressed immaculately in a suave James Bond suit; his widow's peak hairpiece was imperceptible; he was lightly made up with a gentle Mediterranean tan. That is the only time I found Irene lost for words. She mumbled something as she was introduced and then we got down to work.

The big, tall Scotsman was charming and articulate and was happy to announce that he was about to set up an educational foundation for the young, poor people of Glasgow. I sensed that the security of personal wealth attained by playing James Bond had become overwhelmingly important to him. He remained thrifty, so I have been told, but he gave no indication that he was a mean man, as the press have widely reported. Here he was, setting up a charitable organisation for something close to his heart, borne, no doubt, from his own deprived Scottish childhood.

I am always appreciative when a star is co-operative with the TV crew when they visit a film set. It must be difficult for them when they have lines to learn and a myriad of other technicalities to remember, and then give a performance which is captured on celluloid forever. Glenda Jackson was always co-operative, so was Vanessa Redgrave. Not so, Jean Simmons. We had been invited to Shepperton where the director Michael Anderson was making *Dominique* with Miss Simmons in the title role. An interview with the star had been guaranteed by the publicist, otherwise there would have been no point in covering the film. Soon after our arrival we were told that Jean Simmons would not grant us an interview after all. She had learned that morning that her dog in California had died and was distraught. What about that old maxim *the show must go on?* Of course, the show did go on, but not with us.

She had to make an appearance in the movie that afternoon in a large drawing room set. We needed to get a few shots of her in rehearsal to show viewers that the star of the film was, at least, present during our visit. In order to capture those shots, the BBC's 16mm cameraman was dependent upon the studio lighting. Film stars, particularly women, know a great deal about lighting. Jean Simmons certainly did. When she caught a glimpse out of the corner of her eye that our cameraman was poised to capture a shot of her, she immediately walked away and into the darker area beyond the set. She was in only one shot for the actual 'take', which we were not allowed to film because of camera noise. The actress neither looked at us nor spoke to us by way of an apology.

However, the abortive day was saved by two marvellous actors, Cliff Robertson and Dame Flora Robson who were Miss Simmons' co-stars. They were co-operative and pleasant and did all they could to help. They gave good, succinct interviews too. And here is the nub, I think, of Jean Simmons' behaviour. She knew she was not a good interviewee and did not want to subject herself to that indignity. Flora Robson was fun. I did not expect her to be. She was a spinster who lived in Brighton with her two sisters. She saw humour in everything around her and had an endearing chuckle. Everything she said was understated but her turn of phrase and impeccable timing made her an amusing companion. I really warmed to her. She was nothing like the formidable roles she played.

At the MGM studios at Borehamwood, Hertfordshire a Roman street took my fancy for the 1970 remake of Shakespeare's *Julius Caesar*. It had been erected in a large studio. On the Forum steps, Charlton Heston as Mark Antony would make his famous *Friends, Romans, Countrymen* speech. Before the filming of the crucial scene I was able to film interviews in a cramped caravan off stage with Heston and the other male stars - John Gielgud, Jason Robards, Richard Chamberlain and Robert Vaughan. Not bad for a morning's work. The production designer was Julia Trevelyan Oman, better known as a stage and opera designer. She was plain and matronly before her time but enthusiastic about her profession and never dull. She had not yet married the erudite aesthete Roy Strong.

I was fascinated by her sole use of nature's colours in all her designs. For a start, she created in that studio a fantastic perspective so that Roman streets in earthy blues, browns and white, seemed miles away. She showed me her reference files, a meticulous card system which could never be surpassed in today's computer age. On each card was a sample from nature of a particular colour or texture, or both. There were leaves from trees, dried flowers from all manner of plants and samples of sand and soil from beaches, deserts, plains and mountains. I was most impressed. She was a mistress of her art. The finished film is no masterpiece despite its starry cast, but it is worth seeing again if only for the set designs of Miss Trevelyan Oman. It is anybody's guess why she did not become one of Britain's Oscar-winning movie designers. She deserved to be. Instead, she and her husband created a magnificent garden at their Hertfordshire home.

It was now time to film Heston's Mark Antony speech. The extras in togas joined the actors for the rousing scene. While I waited behind the Panavision camera for the director to shout 'action', I praised the wonderful set to the technician beside me. He then told me a true story about the previous film which had been shot on that sound stage. *It was '2001: A Space Odyssey' and we spent £100,000 on a spectacular set made of glass and mirrors. It looked great. The director, Stanley Kubrick walked in, took one look at the finished construction, shook his head and said 'nuh huh' and walked out. The next day,* he said, *the £100,000 unused set was demolished.* After *Julius Caesar* Charlton Heston starred in and this time directed another Shakespearean play *Antony and Cleopatra* with Hildegarde Neil. I always remember *The Guardian* newspaper's review of that film. The headline was *The Biggest Asp Disaster in the World.*

I was always sad when I visited Elstree Studios. The place needed a good overhaul. This was long before the *Star Wars Trilogy* or the *Indiana Jones* series had moved in. The writer/director Bryan Forbes had a short reign as studio head, committed to making low budget British films for the international market. The first three were commercial stinkers but I do not blame him, as others were quick to do. On paper all three looked promising. Roger Moore played a dual role in *The Man Who Haunted Himself;* two promising young actresses, Pamela Franklin and Michele Dotrice starred with the Hungarian actor Sandor Eles in a mystery story set on a cycling holiday in France called *And Soon the Darkness;* the third film Forbes wrote and directed himself, *The Raging Moon* starring his wife Nanette Newman and a young Malcolm McDowell in a romantic drama about a love affair between two inmates of a home for the physically handicapped. Not one of them was a box office success but the losses were not catastrophic. Anyone can make mistakes. Bryan Forbes was ousted soon after. He should have been given another chance.

Some wonderful movies had been made at Elstree, including Britain's first full-length talkie, *Blackmail,* directed by a young Alfred Hitchcock in 1929. In 1969 I was at the same studio to film an insert for my weekly television programme. It was a silly sci-fi yarn called *Moon Zero Two* which featured an almost unknown American actor, James Olsen, and a notable British director, Roy Ward Baker whose career was on the wane. It was the set design which attracted me. The story took place on the Moon in 2021. It was only a couple of months since man had *really* landed on the moon. The designer had incorporated these new images into his set, especially the view of Earth from the Moon. The budget was miniscule - it was a Hammer film - but those sets looked a million dollars, thanks to the ingenuity of British craftsmanship. The studio complex itself needed a total refurbishment. I never returned.

One American producer, Milton Subotstsky who, with his partner Max Rosenberg made low budget horror movies in Britain for their company Amicus Films, gave me some sound advice, *never stint on dressing the set, hire expensive furnishings and good props, get several name stars and pay them well for one or two day's work.* I recall him hiring Sir Ralph Richardson for one day on *Tales from the Crypt.* The film poster announced that he was the star of the movie. Read the cast list for his horror compilation *Asylum* - Peter Cushing, Richard Todd, Robert Powell, Patrick Magee, Britt Ekland, Herbert Lom, Charlotte Rampling and Sylvia Syms. Not bad for a low budget movie.

The best comment on film-making I heard during my countless visits to Britain's major movie studios was on the set of *Carry On Up The Jungle* at Pinewood. I had just returned from my week-long stint in Ireland for the David Lean epic *Ryan's Daughter.* The contrast between the interminable takes on the latter movie on location, and the swift shooting pace on the studio-conceived jungle for this *Carry On* film, was unbelievable. Don't get me wrong, each method was right and proper for the scale and budget of each film. But after seeing director Lean request 'take' after 'take' to achieve perfection, I was amused to hear the *Carry On* director, Gerald Thomas, make the perfect remark after the first 'take' of Terry Scott as Tarzan. Terry had landed somewhat precariously after swinging through the trees, *that'll do, print!*

Barry Brown TV publicity portrait
Sydney, Australia 1957

Barry recording for ABC Radio in India, 1964

Barry at BBC World Service,
Bush House, London 1967

David Niven in Rome with interviewer
Barry Brown and researcher Sheldon Larry
1970

Kirk Douglas filming *Catch Me A Spy,*
in Oban, Scotland 1971

Michael Caine being
interviewed by Tony Bilbov
with director Barry Brown
beside him, Cannes Film
Festival, 1975

Dustin Hoffman and
co-star Valerie Perrine at
the Press Conference for
Lenny, Cannes Film
Festival 1975

Tony Bilbow filming a
piece-to-camera, Cannes
Film Festival, 1975,
watched by director
Barry Brown and
P.A. Sally Stockford

Barry Brown and Barry Norman at Pink Panther Weekend,
Gstaad, Switzerland, 1975

Barry Brown, Gene Wilder, Barry Norman
in Los Angeles, 1975

KATHARINE HOUGHTON HEPBURN

II - 3 - 1977

Dear Barry Brown

      I am sorry.
I simply haven't the time. Thank
you for asking me.

Rejection letter from
Katharine Hepburn,
1977 - at least I tried!

Director Howard Hawks being
filmed in Palm Springs, 1977, for
The Hollywood Greats

British actress Anna Neagle
in 1977 for *The Hollywood Greats*

Clint Eastwood, Barry Brown,
Barry Norman, New York 1977
(notice the Donegal tweed suit!)

Barry Brown interviews
Michael Douglas,
New York 1979

June Allyson, still looking great aged 62
in Santa Barbara, 1979, for
The Hollywood Greats

Zeppo, the youngest of the
Marx Bros. in Palm Springs 1979
for *The Hollywood Greats*

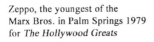

Candice Bergen at
BBC TV Centre, 1981,
with producer Barry Brown,
director Ann Freer and
interviewer Iain Johnstone

Show Business presenter
Mike Smith with PA
Danuta Stancyzk, Producers
Bruce Thompson, Jane Lush
and Programme Editor
Barry Brown, BBC1 1983

HRH Prince Charles,
Prince of Wales,
Barry Norman &
Barry Brown at Guildhall,
London, at BFI 50th
Anniversary Dinner 1983.
(In background, Tony
Smith, Director British
Film Institute)

Fourteen   Jenks & Bilbow

I have mentioned Tony Bilbow quite often. As a long standing presenter of BBC2s *Late Night Line-Up*, he was seconded to *Film Night* and was its chief presenter. Occasionally, Joan Bakewell and Michael Dean stepped in and when Tony had a break from the programme for a couple of years, Sheridan Morley was anchorman. They presented the core of the programme which dealt with current movies but the final 10 minutes was given over to Philip Jenkinson to present his vintage slot. He became quite a household name and wrote a *Radio Times* film column for many years. He had been a film editor, was passionate about old movies and was an avid collector.

Philip passed on his innate enthusiasm to viewers, a neat contrast to the more urbane and cynical Bilbow. *Film Night* emanated from a tiny BBC studio. Because of its size, it was difficult to pair Tony and Philip in one combined set, so they sat separately. Every now and then I would discuss changes with the allocated set designer so that the programme would seem more co-ordinated. The designer was usually inexperienced - the good ones got the big dramas and variety shows in the larger studios. I soon learned that what looked good on paper from a naïve designer was usually impractical.

On one occasion, if had I accepted a design foisted upon me, the cameras would have had to be placed just outside the studio door. A swift adaptation was necessary. It was also difficult in that tiny area to try to seat the presenters so that monstrous bits of the set did not seem to be growing out of their heads. All I wanted from a designer was to be able to seat the two presenters side by side at separate desks with a softly-lit cyclorama behind them.

One new designer had a brain-wave. He would make two curved desks out of fashionable fibreglass - in orange. On the front of each desk, embossed in silver, would be the *Film Night* logo. Because the weekly programme was transmitted 'live', a telephone was a necessity so that if anything went wrong, the presenters could speak directly to me in the control room. The designer painted a new slim-line phone orange to match his beloved set. Not long afterwards I entered the studio to see the new construction by the new designer.

Tony and Philip were already seated. My heart sank. They looked as if they were in the front seat of a Disneyland ride. The cost of fibreglass then was so prohibitive that I was obliged to use that ill-conceived design for more than two years. Ten years later, long after the set had gone to that giant furniture cave in the sky, I was watching a 'live' current affairs programme and there was the same orange phone beside the anchorman. The BBC had many cost-saving practices, long before accountants and consultants took over the place.

My attempts at integrating the two presenters failed. It was just as well. They were very different in style. Tony wrote his script carefully, almost pedantically. He loved words and used them as literary tools to craft his carefully considered introductions to the various film clips.

Philip Jenkinson, or 'Jenks' as we called him, was a law unto himself. Each week he wrote his script using one cliché after another. Each week I tried to tone down the excesses borne from his enthusiasm without spoiling his screen persona. It made no difference. The following week he would revert to his cliché-ridden ways. My blue pencil diluted the worst of them. And so it went on for eight years. Audiences seemed to love him. While I winced at *one of the rarest pieces of celluloid history; the most dramatic scene ever filmed; the best performance ever on the silver screen,* the viewers believed him. He had an enormous postbag. Requests to show scenes from old favourite movies poured in from all over the country. 'Jenks' had hired a garage or two near his home where he stored his enormous collection of 16mm movies. Each week he would splice the requested clips in their correct sequence, with a piece of film 'leader' between each one. For transmission, the telecine operator would play in the clips on cue.

One Sunday Philip commenced his 'live' slot. During the first clip the film snapped. There was no time to repair the damage. The remaining 'inserts' for the programme were on that same reel of 16mm film. The orange slim-line phone rang in the studio. I told 'Jenks' to ad lib while I decided what to do next. He started rambling on about the clip we would have shown. I rang again and told him to continue talking while I alerted the on-duty Editor for BBC2 that the programme would be finishing early. I was grateful for Philip's next cliché - he made some mention of *circumstances beyond our control.* Just then another phone in the control room rang. It was my departmental head, Rowan Ayers calling from home, *get that bloody programme off the air* he bellowed. That was precisely what I was desperately trying to do. The rest of that evening's programme was abandoned. In years of 'live' transmissions of *Film Night,* that was my worst disaster.

Later, when my TV colleagues said they preferred the excitement of 'live' TV to the safety of pre-recorded TV, I always leapt to the defence of the latter. I *hated* 'live' TV.

I did it weekly for 5 ½ years. I was glad when videotape became more economical and we could record our topical programme earlier in the day, edit it and present to viewers a truly polished programme. I know 'Jenks' and Bilbow liked the buzz of a 'live' show. Viewers do too - they love to see things go wrong. That is why 'out-take' programmes are so popular. Recently I saw the out-take from an interview with an American boxer after his big match. *What state were in you after the fight,* asked the interviewer. His reply was a gem - *South Dakota.*

'Jenks' had good contacts in many areas of the film industry. This enabled him to show an infinite variety of vintage movie clips at little or no cost to the programme. One of his greatest achievements was to introduce British audiences to the extraordinary talent of Busby Berkeley, the Hollywood choreographer whose lavish production numbers in black-and-white movies were the epitome of 'camp'. The choreographer adored women and featured them prominently on those huge Hollywood sound stages. He created incredible kaleidoscopic patterns by using overhead cameras. He was one of the first to do so and no one outshone him. You only have to watch *Gold Diggers of 1933 and 1935, Footlight Parade* and *Dames* to witness a genius at work.

Anyone who watched *Film Night* will know about Busby Berkeley, but they will pronounce his surname as "Bark-ley", because 'Jenks' said it that way. Any American will tell you it is pronounced as "Berk-ley". A whole nation has Philip Jenkinson to blame for this mispronunciation. It was indicative of this presenter's widespread influence and popularity at the time.

'Jenks" went to Hollywood in 1968 and returned having filmed interviews with silent stars Ramon Navarro and Gloria Swanson and directors Rouben Mamoulian and John Ford. Consequently, *Film Night* must have been the only TV programme in the world to broadcast a topical interview with Navarro the day after he had been murdered in November 1968.

Jenks' was not a good interviewer but he was tenacious. His banal questioning turned John Ford into one of the most cantankerous interviewees ever. Philip was the polite Englishman with a slight Northern accent; Ford was the typical, tough, macho Irish-American. I detected an obvious clash of personalities but it made good television. The director emphasised during that interview that it was he who had made John Wayne a movie star. It was he who had whisked him away from playing bit parts in 'B' movies to take the leading role in *Stagecoach*. Thank heavens the cowboy changed his name. He was christened Marion Michael Morrison.

A couple of weeks after his return from the States, Philip travelled to Sussex to interview Boris Karloff, then 81 years old. Although his career had flourished in the USA, he was born in England in 1887 as William Henry Pratt. He had returned to spend his final years in the country of his birth. He was a diffident, charming man with a gentle, cultured, voice. It is a pity that he is remembered only as the monster in *Frankenstein*.

Other interviews 'Jenks' instigated during my regime were with two Hollywood composers Dimitri Tiomkin, who wrote wonderful scores for *Lost Horizon, High Noon, Giant, The Old Man and The Sea* and the memorable whistling theme for *The High and the Mighty;* and Miklos Rozsa, who was responsible for such classics as *Spellbound, Lust for Life* and *Ben Hur*.

When Maurice Chevalier, still a handsome man at 84, came to London to promote his final autobiography *I Remember It Well,* 'Jenks' made sure he would be interviewed on *Film Night*. When perky Debbie Reynolds, star of *Singin' in the Rain*, visited London privately to see her daughter, Carrie Fisher who was then studying at the Central School of Speech and Drama, Philip arranged to film an interview with her. Trust him to know that she was in town. His contribution to *Film Night* was considerable and I learned a great deal from him. He was often temperamental but he was generous to a fault and an ardent hypochondriac. His shoulder bag was portable pharmacy, which the rest of the production team found useful at times.

I am grateful to Tony Bilbow for urging me to change the regular format of the show. As I have mentioned already, the programme was dependent upon the willingness of film distribution companies to provide movie clips. Without them there would be no *Film Night*. The same was true of a rival programme on ITV called *Cinema*, hosted then by Michael Parkinson. Both programmes publicised current movies in return for free use of pre-selected clips. As a quid pro quo, the companies would, if needed, delve into their archives to provide scenes from past feature films to complement interviews with stars or to develop a programme theme, like cops and robbers, or the Hollywood musical. No copyright costs would be incurred so it was rather cheap programming.

On the commercial channel Parkinson wrote a nifty script and sometimes made a subtle hint that a film might not be all that is was cracked up to be. At the BBC we had gone one step further by persuading some distributors to allow us to choose our own clips. Not all were prepared to play ball but it was a step in the right direction.

One day Tony suggested he review a film rather than just give details of cast and plot. It did not concern him what the implications might be, he was not the producer. I agreed to give it a go, but with only one or two reviews per programme. The film companies did not seem to mind when he gave a movie a favourable review, but when it was unfavourable, they were up in arms. This was 1969 and no movie reviewing had yet begun on American TV, so no precedent had been set.

Most of the British companies were subsidiaries of giant
US distributors e.g. United Artists, Columbia, Warner Bros.
20th Century Fox, MGM etc. This was groundbreaking stuff
and they would have none of it. One by one, the companies
refused to provide clips for the programme. Each time this
would happen, Tony would end his review by saying *we
would like to show you a scene from this film, but the distributors,
United Artists* (or whoever) *have refused.* Now the reverse
happened. They were furious that, because of their ban, no
clip would be shown when Tony gave one of their movies
a good review. So the ban would be lifted by, say, United
Artists, but then MGM would refuse clips because of a bad
review. And so it went on, swings and roundabouts for
months. I was worried. Tony seemed delighted at his on air
stance but it did not make good television.

To my mind, more people tuned in to see clips of new
movies rather than to hear what Tony had to say about
them. If we announced that no clips would be shown, there
was a 'talking head' on screen for far too long. So I was
pleased when Tony leaked our dilemma to a journalist.
British newspapers took up the cudgels on our behalf. This
helped but did not resolve the situation. Those British bosses
had American bosses and many were reluctant to rock the
boat.

The next Bond film was about to be released. I was in dispute
with United Artists, the distributor of the movie. Therefore
I approached the production company, Eon Films, and they
provided the necessary material. This annoyed United
Artists even more. Eventually the matter was resolved but
not before I had endured a most uneasy lunch with United
Artists' UK Head of Publicity.

I continued to tread warily, to be diplomatic towards the
distributors whose favours were needed to provide all kinds
of clips, not only their current movies. I knew it entailed
a great deal of effort on their part to make this material
available and, remember, no charge was made for this

service. Presenters do not think like producers, and I know that Sheridan Morley, during his tenure, became frustrated when I asked him not to review a certain film, just introduce it until the programme's relationship with that particular distributor was on a firmer footing.

I regret that *Film Night* never reached the stage where it could review *all* the movies featured in the programme until after Tony and Sheridan had left. I was not courageous enough. It took my colleague and friend, Iain Johnstone, to pave the way when he started a regional programme on BBC 1 for London and the South East only, called *Film 71* with the journalist Jackie Gillott as its first critic.

By 1975 the new Controller of BBC2, Aubrey Singer, had become a severe critic of *Film Night.* He did not appreciate the presentation skills of either Tony Bilbow or Philip Jenkinson and eventually instructed me not to renew their contracts. It is hard to tell those you have worked with for many years that they are not wanted any more, particularly as they had families and mortgages.

They were freelance and I was a member of BBC staff. My job was secure. Consequently, they blamed me for their fall from grace and I can understand their displeasure. Unknown to Tony, for the next ten months I made sure his casual work for the programme, a fortnightly interview, paid him exactly the same sum he had received while he was under contract. It was the best I could do but it took him a long time to forgive me. He and Philip were part of an era that has long since passed.

To ring the changes to *Film Night*, I engaged three reviewers to appear fortnightly. They were the movie journalist David Castell, the journalist and film publicist; Jane Mercer from the British Film Institute; and Chris Petit, the *Time Out* magazine film critic. They were chosen after rigorous auditions. This process is just as much an ordeal for the producer as it is for the potential presenters but no one would believe that. It is a tremendous burden to bear. Did you make the right decision and choose the best?

This trio would please the Controller of BBC 2, or so I thought. They were young and bright with a good knowledge of movies. They would review the latest films from a younger person's perspective. They were inexperienced on camera but they would soon improve. Wrong. They appeared on TV once a fortnight for a few minutes to review a film from a script on autocue. It was not a simple task and the trio had little time to gain experience. Those with a natural talent make it look easy, but it is not.

Over six months, David Castell improved his performance slightly, Jane Mercer stayed exactly the same, and Chris Petit got worse. I was miserable.

In alternate weeks there was the Bilbow interview and some were more interesting than others. One was with the American director of *The Vikings, Tora, Tora Tora* and *Doctor Dolittle*, Richard Fleischer, whose father, Max, had produced all those Popeye cartoons I had loved so much as a child.

I have two memories of that interview. First Fleischer explained how, when editing a movie he has just shot, he notices that one knowing glance between two characters on screen can make the next two pages of dialogue redundant; the producers then chide him for wasting their money filming an unnecessary scene. Secondly, he explained how in the cutting room he edits his movies, making them shorter and crisper until the pace is right and the story is succinct - in other words he has the movie at just the length he wants it, knowing that nothing more can be deleted without ruining it.

The movie is then given trial screenings at cinemas in and around Los Angeles. After getting the audiences' written reaction at those previews, he always returns to the cutting room and deletes another 20 minutes. I only wish more of today's movie makers followed that maxim.

By March 1976, Aubrey Singer had had enough. In his opinion the Tony Bilbow interviews all had the same old ring to them; the three new presenters had not improved. He wrote me a memo on his Controller BBC2 note paper announcing that *Film Night* would not return in the autumn. I was ready to move on to other things.

During my long association with the programme I had created, the most fun I had was when I decided to show unintentional double entendres from vintage movies. For several weeks it became an obsession, as the production team viewed countless movies trying to find the most appropriate rude scenes. Viewers also wrote in with their suggestions. My favourite was from Fred Astaire and Ginger Roger's final RKO movie together *The Story of Vernon and Irene Castle*. They were on tour in Holland doing a spot of window shopping. Suddenly Ginger noticed a shop selling traditional costumes. She turned to Fred and said *I've always wanted a little Dutch cap!*

Fifteen   The Other Barry

I first met Barry Norman at the end of the 1960s. The Hollywood comic actor Jerry Lewis was launching to the media a chain of family-oriented cinemas in Britain. He wanted good, decent movies all the family could see together in his cinemas. He emphasised how proud he was of his six sons and his happy marriage. Therefore, it came as no surprise when a few years later his marriage broke up and he was accused of being a cocaine addict. His dream of a movie-house chain, which flourished for a time in the USA, never saw the light of day in Britain.

I had never liked silly Jerry Lewis on screen. He was too frantic to be funny. Only in 1997 when I saw him in the West End playing the lead in the musical *Damn Yankees* did I realise what a superb performer he was. His portrayal was understated and subtle, he knew every stage trick in the book and used them effectively. He was simply great as the Devil incarnate.

Barry Norman was at that Press Conference as Show Business Editor of *The Daily Mail*. When it was merged with the now defunct *Daily Star* in 1971, he was made redundant. His wife, Diana, who was writing a book on astrology, phrenology, and several other 'ologys', arranged for him to have his palm read. The palmist was most prescient. She told him *you will be very successful but not in your chosen profession*. This was devastating news for a dyed-in-the wool journalist who had worked his way up from local cub reporter, preferring a career in newspapers to a University degree.

I noticed that Barry, by now a freelance journalist, wrote the occasional TV review in *The Times*. This led to an invitation to appear on BBC2's *Late Night Line-Up* in a discussion about that evening's TV output. Around this time the producer Iain Johnstone was using guest presenters for six weeks at a time on his BBC1 programme *Film 71* which, as I have already mentioned, was broadcast only in London and South East England. I remember seeing journalist Irma Kurtz and writer Frederic Raphael doing their stints. I watched it regularly because it was wholly a film review programme, albeit local, whereas I was treading carefully on my national film slot with only occasional reviews.

Iain, who had chosen the best ever TV signature tune for this programme - Billy Taylor playing *I Wish I Knew How It Would Feel To Be Free* - now made another wise choice. He invited Barry Norman to present *Film 72* for six weeks. Barry did the job so well that he stayed for 26 years. By the end of 1972 Iain, a typical Aries, wanted to move on. He confided to me once that he liked starting programmes but quickly tired of producing them. So he went off to start the current affairs programme *Midweek* choosing once more an excellent signature tune. With other producers at the helm, *Film 72, 73 and 74* flourished. During the spring run of *Film 75* the contract of its current producer was not renewed. It was unfair but not of my doing.

The then Controller of BBC1, Bryan Cowgill, encouraged by Barry Norman's effortless presenting skills, asked if I would start producing *Film 75* from September onwards in an endeavour to improve it sufficiently so that he could schedule it as a national rather than the regional programme it now was. That is how I started an 8 year working relationship with 'the other Barry'. To avoid confusion he started calling me *Bazza* which he does to this day.

The production team, the same as for *Film Night,* worked doubly hard with our new-found presenter. I was pleased to be working on TV with a former hard-nosed journalist with a witty way with words. People used to ask me *does Barry Norman make up what he says as he goes along?* I was always flabbergasted at this preposterous suggestion. Barry had usually less than two minutes to tell the plot and give his opinion of the film he was reviewing. I challenge anyone to come out of a cinema and ad lib his or her critique to me in under two minutes. *Of course* he wrote his script beforehand, giving himself time to simplify or embellish his pertinent phrases. One of my favourites was when he was reviewing an unsuccessful Faye Dunaway movie *The Eyes of Laura Mars.* At one point he exclaimed, *and there was Faye Dunaway Faye Dingaway.* Brilliant.

After four weeks on air with the revamped *Film 75,* Bryan Cowgill rang me direct, rare for a Controller of BBC1 who usually contacted the departmental head. He said: *The programme's heading in the right direction. It will be transmitted all over the UK from April 1976.* That was the start of Barry Norman becoming a national TV icon. I realised quite early on that he did not need much rehearsal. If he did, he became irritated and grew stale. He remembered almost word for word what he had written but it was always copied onto autocue for him to read. If ever I altered just one word of his script, he always fluffed it at rehearsal. He wrote rhythmically and broke all the rules of TV writing. Short, crisp sentences are best. Barry wrote long, complex ones using such words as *former* and *latter* which I had been taught were for correspondence, not TV. It worked for him.

Perhaps I should explain how the autocue works. A small TV screen device is fitted below the lens of the TV camera on which is printed the text for the programme. An angled mirror then reflects the words on to the camera lens. The operator, who sits at the side of the studio, uses a tiny machine to feed the lines of the script at the pace of the presenter. Inexperienced performers, who struggle with autocue, invariably complain that the operator is going too fast! Not Barry. He did not need to peer at the screen. He set the pace without flinching and the operator followed. That was his gift.

In order to keep the programme fresh, I decreed that Barry Norman would have only one run-through at rehearsal, some fine-tuning would take place, then the programme would be recorded for transmission that evening. After all, he was a journalist, not an actor. To achieve this, the script had to be prepared like an orchestral score. Absolutely everything had to be written down, nothing left to chance. I was a firm believer in organised spontaneity, this was gospel. The script would not be printed until every film or videotape cue had been included; until every numbered photograph, film poster or 35mm slide had been described accurately; until the duration of every section of the programme had been listed; until every camera shot had been designated.

Just before each rehearsal the technicians in the studio and in the film and videotape areas in other parts of TV Centre were given their scripts with their appropriate duties clearly marked. The run-through would be similar to a concert at London's Royal Festival Hall. I was the conductor, Barry the soloist, the studio director was leader of the orchestra and everyone else the musicians. The run-through was usually pretty good. A few amendments were made and shortly afterwards the programme would be recorded, as planned.

It sounds like a rigid procedure but I could be flexible, when necessary. I have always believed in having a plan, then, when something needs changing, I can see how it affects everything else. That is my way of working. Other successful producers leave all their options open and then make brilliant last-minute decisions. To my mind, the stress created by that method for everyone connected with the production is simply not worth it. Once I went to a party and when someone heard that I was a BBC producer, asked me what I liked most about producing. I pondered then replied, *'I love making order out of chaos.*

How strange, he replied, *most BBC producers I know love making chaos out of order!*

.The first overseas trip Barry and I made together was soon after the launch of the new-look *Film 75.* Sir Lew Grade, who had entertained me at that Press luncheon at the Hotel du Cap a few years earlier, was now delighted by the box office success of his investment in *The Return of the Pink Panther,* thus heralding another spate of comedies featuring Peter Sellers as the hapless Inspector Clouseau. I had filmed a report for the programme about the making of this film on location near Nice the previous summer. Mr. Sellers, who had been so uncooperative during *Alice's Adventures in Wonderland,* gave a jokey interview after a superb lunch - French location caterers are the best in the world.

At the same location, I had also managed to film interviews with the other stars of the movie Christopher Plummer and Catherine Schell and the director Blake Edwards. This item, when transmitted, certainly drew attention to the movie and may have played some part in its success. Anyway, the film company hosted a thank you party for the world's press at Gstaad, Switzerland, one of the world's most fashionable resorts. It was to be *A Pink Weekend.*

Because of recording commitments, Barry and I could not fly to Geneva with the rest of the invited journalists, so we caught an early evening flight instead. We were collected at Geneva airport and driven through spectacular mountain scenery to Gstaad's premier hotel, The President. We dashed to a welcome party which included a disco. The director Blake Edwards and his wife, Julie Andrews, were at the top table, so as I knew their personal assistant Tony Adams from that visit to Nice, I sat with him and Peter Sellers' two teenage children whom he seemed to ignore the entire weekend. Also in the party was Emma Walton, Julie's 12 year old daughter by her first marriage to the talented production designer Tony Walton. Quite early on, Tony asked Emma to dance. I was stunned by her sophisticated reply. After all, she was not yet a teenager.

A little later, perhaps?

Look Emma, replied Tony brusquely, *you either dance with me now or not at all*

Emma rose immediately. No wonder Irish-born Tony Adams won promotion. He became Associate, then Producer on all Blake Edwards' future movies.

At the end of the evening, when we reached our adjacent rooms, Barry and I noticed a pile of gifts outside our doors. Each was wrapped in pink paper. There was a fondue set, a Swiss pen, and a box of chocolates. The company PR man had organised some wonderful freebies from Swiss manufacturers for all the guests.

I was awakened early in the morning by cowbells. I looked out my hotel window. It was picture postcard perfect. Breakfast and all subsequent meals were superb. The Swiss run everything like clockwork and are at their best in hotel management. Later the same day, the other Barry approached me looking distressed. *What's the matter?* I enquired.

I am suffering withdrawal symptoms, twenty minutes have passed and no new pink presents have been left outside my door. It was that kind of a weekend.

The highlight was the Saturday evening Gala Dinner. Beside each name plate was yet another pink present - a Swiss watch.

I mentioned earlier that Richard Burton and Elizabeth Taylor were seated at the next table. I tried not to gawp. On stage a local Swiss band played somewhat enthusiastically. Apparently, Miss Taylor announced that if the music did not stop she would leave. Peace at last.

We retired after the sumptuous meal to a covered patio for the evening's cabaret. It was Henry Mancini and his Orchestra with guest artist Julie Andrews, dressed, of course, in pink. The haunting *Pink Panther* theme was even more evocative when conducted by the composer himself. I was given a task to perform which I shall always treasure. Blake Edwards and Julie Andrews were seated in front of me for the concert and when it was time for Julie to sing, I had to hand her the microphone. She acknowledged with a smile, the nearest I ever got to meeting her. In Australia I had played the original stage cast recording of *My Fair Lady* featuring Julie Andrews as Eliza Doolittle at least 120 times and I had adored her as the cheeky Maria in the movie version of *The Sound of Music*. Here she was in the flesh with her peaches and cream complexion, well groomed dark blond hair, even prettier in real life than on the screen.

On Sunday before our departure for the airport, Sir Lew made a speech thanking us for attending and announced the current world wide box office receipts for his Pink Panther movie. We should have been thanking him.

I have already mentioned our other trip to Basle in Switzerland to interview Sophia Loren making *The Cassandra Crossing*. In the hotel bar during that visit I met one of the supporting actors of that movie. He was black, tall, good looking and muscular. He had been a football star, then an advertising model for Hertz cars and now he was a budding film star. His name was O.J. Simpson. He was easy to talk to but you could tell he was bored in this pretty Swiss town. He told me how much he had been looking forward to getting away from America where everyone recognised him wherever he went. Now, after two weeks, he was missing the attention. At least he was honest. Years later, did he or did he not kill his wife and her friend? I was not surprised when he was acquitted. He was so charming he could get away with murder.

We also filmed an interview with Sophia Loren's co-star, Richard Harris, a hellraiser if ever I met one, but always eager to please a TV crew and perform for the cameras. He was a big man and extremely likeable, well, most drinkers are, but now he was behaving himself.

I was also glad to spend some time with another actor in the film, Lee Strasberg. He had founded the famous Actors' Studio which introduced Method Acting to America in the 1950s and had Marilyn Monroe as one of his pupils. More recently he had made a great impact as a film actor in *The Godfather Part II* and on the strength of that had been offered a part in *The Cassandra Crossing*. He only made 5 movies before he died in 1982. He was 77 when I met him, a tiny man with brown eyes, a permanent tan and full of wisdom about the art of acting. It was how he expressed himself rather than what he said which made you listen. I hung on to every word he uttered. The other Barry was intrigued too. He agreed to film an interview for our programme although that had not been my original intention. It was fascinating stuff.

Back in England in the *Film 76* cutting room it became apparent that the Lee Strasberg interview could not be part of the location report. It was about acting, rather than *The Cassandra Crossing*. I intended to edit it later and transmit it separately. I did not make this point clear to the film editor so when the edited location item had been transmitted, he junked all the off-cuts, all the pieces of unused footage. Accidentally, the whole of the Lee Strasberg interview was lost for posterity. It could have been a treasure in the BBC archives.

Quite early on in our working relationship, Barry and I were invited by 20th Century Fox to Long Beach, California on a world-wide junket to promote the world premieres of two movies *The Adventure of Sherlock Holmes' Smarter Brother* and *Lucky Lady.* We weren't to know that they were going to be box office turkeys, nor did the studio. The film company took over the former Cunard liner *Queen Mary,* so for two nights we had the luxury of sleeping in grandeur aboard a permanently moored ship now used as a tourist attraction. Apart from the cabins, the dining room and ballroom were still intact but the decks were filled with downmarket tat. My cabin had wonderful mahogany wood panelling and the bath was almost the size of a children's swimming pool. The old fashioned, enormous taps and plug looked as if they had been invented by Heath Robinson.

This was my first visit to the USA and on the drive up to Los Angeles, Barry pointed out *Pickfair* to me, the former home of silent stars Douglas Fairbanks Snr and Mary Pickford who, with Charlie Chaplin and director D.W. Griffith were the founders of United Artists. Our first stop was the 20th Century Fox Studios, which in itself was awe-inspiring. The entrance now boasted part of the New York set for *Hello Dolly* made there 7 years earlier. We joined many US TV presenters on the set of *The Duchess and the Dirtwater Fox* (another turkey) and met its stars Goldie Hawn and George Segal, who were available for interviews. It was fascinating to see how the Americans interviewed their stars - the local TV presenters felt they were just as important as their guests. They sat beside them to record their interviews whereas in Britain, the star is the focus of attention and the interviewer has his back to the camera.

One TV presenter from a Milwaukee station talked to George Segal about George's family's interest in the local brewery. George confirmed this and they chatted most jovially about it. The movie was not even mentioned. There was no depth or thought given to any of the interviews I watched being recorded, everything was sweetness and light - and bland. I could not get over how gorgeous Goldie Hawn was. She was tall, slim and blonde with huge kewpie-doll blue eyes and a flawless complexion. She was charming, funny and unfazed by the whole experience. She was one of life's 'copers', you could tell.

After that we were driven to interview Gene Wilder and Marty Feldman, stars of the Sherlock Holmes movie. It was Wilder's first time as writer, star and director. After screening it I thought it should have been his last but he redeemed himself a decade later with *Woman in Red* which was far less self-indulgent. The irony was that we went all the way to California to interview the two stars, when the actual film had been shot earlier in the year at Shepperton Studios just outside London.

Whenever we filmed an interview with Marty Felman, the goggle-eyed English comic, he always played the same trick. It was tedious. As I've mentioned, a clapper board is used just as filming begins so that picture and sound can be synchronised later in the cutting room. Marty would dash from his chair, grab the clapper board from the technician and do it himself - rather irritating. He then proceeded to be outrageous, a common trait with insecure entertainers. Gene Wilder was marginally more interesting but I never warmed to him either. He was endearing on screen in a manic, vulnerable way, but he lacked warmth as an interviewee.

Lucky Lady had different problems. We had not seen a preview of this movie in London so we were taken by bus once more to the 20th Century Fox studios where we dined in the commissary. Burt Reynolds, one of the movie's stars, made an appearance towards the end of the meal. I was impressed by his almost authentic hairpiece. The others, Gene Hackman and Liza Minnelli were nowhere to be seen, but the teenage actor Robby Benson, who played a supporting role in the movie, stayed on board the *Queen Mary* the whole weekend. Film actors treat their promotional and public duties quite differently when they are on the way up.

The final scene of *Lucky Lady,* which Barry Norman and I saw that evening was not the one shown in cinemas. Hackman, Minnelli and Reynolds were old and living in splendour in Rome, enjoying the spoils of their rum-running activities. Apparently, three endings were filmed at a cost of an extra half million dollars to the movie's already substantial budget. They had try-out screenings with preview audiences and settled for the least worst. Understandably, the director, Stanley Donen, did not mention this expensive hiccup when we had interviewed him earlier in the day. He was there to publicise the movie and all was sweetness and light.

On the Saturday evening rumours spread amongst the Press on board that the stars of *Lucky Lady* would not be making their scheduled appearance for interviews. They were upset about the chosen ending for the movie. The executives of 20th Century Fox remained 'mum' whilst still reassuring us that all was well. It was an anxious time for me because when you travel long distances for such an event, the BBC expects you to return with plenty of broadcast material.

It was an even more anxious time for Barry Norman. In the middle of the night he mistook the cabin door for the bathroom. Consequently he found himself locked out, on deck wearing very little. He had to report to the Purser's Office in his state of undress to get another cabin key. Unaware of this incident, I continued to fret about my dilemma. The main reason for going to Long Beach was to obtain promised interviews with the three big stars of *Lucky Lady.* This would be a coup for the first edition of *Film 76* in the New Year. I did not take a film crew with me as US technicians had been allocated to film any interviews needed for foreign TV programmes. All I had to bring with me was the necessary 16mm film stock. I was worried. The only material I had 'in the can' was an interview with the director but not one of its stars.

Early next morning it was announced that the three *Lucky Lady* stars would be flown in by helicopter, express their grievances at a press conference, then depart. I realised no 20th Century Fox film crew would be made available to capture this. A production team from ZDF in Germany, no doubt with a programme budget thrice the size of mine, had brought their own 16mm film crew. They intended to film the Press Conference. I pleaded with them to print up two copies of what they shot and air freight the extra one to me from Germany. And so I got my 'coup' for *Film 76*.

With hindsight it was hardly worth the effort. The movie received poor reviews and limped along at the box office, despite the engaging performances by its stars. It was an unlucky trip. After an eleven hour flight home, there was freezing fog at Heathrow so we were advised that the plane would be diverted to Manchester. When the passengers were told this news, the director Michael Winner, ensconced in First Class, came meandering down to us in Economy and simply asked, *where is Manchester?* He had a car to meet him which whisked him back to London. He did not offer us a lift so we were bundled by bus to Piccadilly Station in Manchester where, after a long wait, British Rail put us into unheated, dingy carriages and gave us a free Coke and a Cadbury's chocolate roll. We arrived back in London on a freezing December day at 2pm, eight hours later than scheduled. Who said working in TV was glamorous?

Barry Norman and I had a more pleasant time when we were invited to attend the 1976 Tehran Film Festival. An Iranian crew was on hand to film any interviews we wanted plus any atmospheric shots of their city. As Tehran is a rather unpleasant place with the world's worst traffic congestion, I used very little footage on filming shots of the Iranian capital itself. Also I did not trust the inexperienced Iranians to provide movie clips of Festival films whilst I was there, so

I did my homework and made sure they would be available in London on my return. Anything I managed to achieve in Tehran was a bonus, rather than a necessity, so I could relax a little on this trip.

The Shah of Iran was Head of State and his sister gave a reception at her Palace on the outskirts of town. Our bus had a police motorcycle escort, otherwise we would not have arrived before midnight. When we did arrive there was a kerfuffle. We were at the wrong Palace. It was the Shah's mother's palace, not his sister's. We travelled on. It was in these sumptuous surroundings that I met Rita Moreno, who had won a Best Supporting Oscar for her role in *West Side Story* in 1961. Her latest movie was scheduled for the Festival and she was to make a public appearance. It was called *The Ritz* and set in a gay New York bathhouse with Rita playing a talentless Puerto Rican singer who entertains the towelled clientele with songs from Broadway shows. Was this a movie which audiences in this Muslim country would relate to? Bright and bubbly Rita did not seem to mind. She was there on an all-expenses-paid publicity trip with her doctor husband in tow. She was there to do her job and she did it.

The following evening Barry and I attended the festival screening of *The Ritz*. We viewed it in English with Persian sub-titles. Consequently the audience chuckled ten seconds after Barry and I had let out a huge guffaw. Rita's rendition of *Everything's Coming Up Roses* from *Gypsy* in a strong Puerto Rican accent, having broken the heel of one shoe, was hilarious. The Festival audience loved it.

The director of *The Ritz*, Richard Lester, was also in Tehran with his wife. I had arranged for the local film crew to set up outside the downtown Festival Office so that we could interview the director in daylight, without the need for TV lighting. Just as Barry was about to start the interview, we all had to dash for our lives. We noticed that a car was careering along the pavement. Out of sheer frustration at the gridlock in this prominent Tehran street a driver had taken the law into his own hands. He decided to travel along the pavement rather than wait ten more minutes to turn right at the next corner. It was a shock for us all, but Richard Lester was his usual amusing self during the ensuing interview, as if nothing untoward had happened.

We were overjoyed when the Festival organisers offered their guests a free, two-day air tour to Isfahan and Shiraz, culminating with a visit to Persepolis, the capital of ancient Persia which had been ransacked by Alexander the Great in 330BC. Those who were available and wished to participate had to put their names down on a list. I did so immediately and so did 25 others. When we set off on a scheduled flight to our first destination, I was pleased that Richard Lester and his wife were in the row in front. At least there was someone we knew. Richard looked at the 'In Flight' magazine. It was in Persian. He reached the crossword puzzle, turned around to me and said with a broad grin *what's 6 Up?* No wonder the Beatles had chosen him to launch them on their quirky movie career with *A Hard Day's Night* in 1964.

At Isfahan airport we got into a waiting bus. Our fellow passengers were a prestigious bunch. Apart from the Lesters, there was the Hollywood director Arthur Hiller who had had a great hit in 1970 with *Love Story*. In the next row was the willowy blonde actress Sally Kellerman who had made a name for herself as the sexy nurse in the 1970 Robert Altman movie M*A*S*H and had just made *The Big Bus*. At the front of the coach, was the British actress Rita Tushingham, best remembered for *A Taste of Honey*. With her was Ousama Rawi, her cinematographer boyfriend.

When we reached our hotel, we, the two Barrys, were given a bedroom to share. Fair enough. Then Barry Norman saw the double bed. *I've heard about sleeping with the producer, but this is ridiculous,* he commented. No doubt the name *Barry* had suggested to the Iranian authorities in charge of the tour, that we were a married couple. Back in reception we changed to a room with twin beds. The tour of Isfahan was wonderful in such exulted company and I was particularly impressed by the famous Blue Mosque adorned by millions of mosaic tiles and gold leaf.

I was more impressed by Rita Tushingham. She is a funny lady. I was telling her about a friend of mine who was becoming increasingly deaf. Quick as a flash she said *Pardon?* I started to repeat myself - it took me a second or two to get the joke. For the past 20 years I have played the same trick on others. Thanks Rita. She also had a unique party piece. She could close one eye, making her eyelid completely flat, not crinkled up like most people. It looked hilarious. From then on during the tour, I tried whenever I could grab a spare moment to practise the same trick, so that I too could shut one eye like Rita.

When the plane landed at Shiraz it was quite frightening. The power of the Shah was evident with a display of at least 100 military helicopters on the tarmac. Military guards were everywhere with machine guns or revolvers at the ready. We forgot about this oppressive atmosphere when we toured Persepolis. The ancient ruined architecture was overwhelming, tall and powerful yet beautiful and proud.

The tour guide told us she had been photographed with Elizabeth Taylor during her recent visit. The same guide had no idea there were other Hollywood film stars and directors in her midst - as well as a BBC TV personality and his producer! On the direct flight back to Tehran, the other Barry sat with Rita and Ousama, I had a window seat in the row behind. The two remaining seats were empty. Not long after take-off a burly, swarthy Iranian military guard, revolver at his side, sat in the aisle seat. Why does one feel guilty when someone in authority sits near you? I watched the countryside until dark when a light meal was served. After dinner I noticed my reflection in the plane's window. I thought this would be a good chance to practise Rita's eyelid trick. I was winking away to my heart's content when suddenly I noticed the military guard's reflection. It looked as if I were winking at him. I cannot swear it but I thought I saw him reach for his gun.

When we returned to London Barry Norman exclaimed, *that's the best package holiday I've ever had.*

Sixteen   Bazza At Large

There were times when the other Barry was so busy viewing
the week's movies, writing his script, then his *Radio Times*
column, recording a commentary for a location report and
answering his fan mail, that I had to go on location without
him. If any filming took place, I edited out my questions
and collated a sequence of answers, leaving space for Barry
to add a commentary later. In that way it established the
programme as Barry Norman's own.

One cool summer day I took a BBC film crew to a disused
school in South London where Glenda Jackson and Oliver
Reed were making *The Class of Miss MacMichael*. Glenda
played the role of dedicated teacher to a class of social misfits,
no doubt in preparation for a future role in British politics.
Oliver Reed was the uncaring, conservative headmaster.
He looked the role and gave no indication that he might be
dying for a drink at the end of the day. He duly received
many column inches of free publicity in the tabloids but I
never saw him drunk on a film set.

The director was the Canadian, Silvio Narizzano who had
made *Georgy Girl* and *Loot*. I had prepared my questions
carefully so as not to waste time when the actors became

available between scenes. I wish I had prepared my route map more carefully. I got hopelessly lost driving there. It is so unprofessional to turn up late, particularly when your film crew is punctual. They had already stuffed themselves with bacon sandwiches and coffee, a prerequisite on any British movie location. It was a fairly easy working day.

Soon after my arrival we grabbed a couple of good scenes with the leading actors in rehearsal and by mid afternoon had also filmed interviews with both stars, the director and the writer/producer - not using French filters this time as he was quite articulate. I noticed that the distinguished stage actor, John Standing, was also on call that day although the film publicist had not alerted me to this fact. I had prepared no questions for him but it seemed churlish to interview everyone else but him. I decided to 'wing' it. The camera started rolling, the clapperboard was struck and I asked the first question:

Barry: *John Standing, why are you in this movie?*

John: *You may well ask!*

It was a hilarious reply. I had simply wanted to enquire how his role fitted in to the complexities of the plot but it all came out wrong. The other Barry would never have been so oblique. That is why I am such a believer in organised spontaneity.

The star of *An Officer and a Gentleman* and *Terms of Endearment,* Debra Winger, was in town, she with the vulnerable, deep brown eyes and the sexy, deep, husky voice. Debra could only be interviewed on a Sunday and the other Barry was unavailable. I went along instead. We set up the film camera in one room of her suite at Claridge's and she eventually made her entrance, just a little late. I was sadly disappointed. A costume designer and make-up artist can do wonders for a screen heroine. When an actress is left to her own devices, the illusion is sometimes lost.

Debra wore a turquoise taffeta dress with a low waistline, the sort of outfit you would expect a convent girl to wear on her first date. She must have used her own curlers. Her amateurish coiffure made her look ingenuous. She was far from that. There were rumours she was having an affair with a congressman from Nebraska and I am almost certain he was lying low in the next room.

I forgot all about that once the interview began. I was trying to learn about the rivalry which existed between her and Shirley MacLaine, who played her mother in *Terms of Endearment*. The press had been full of it. Recently Shirley had won Best Actress Oscar although both had been nominated for their roles in that tear-jerker. No way would Debra budge. She and Shirley respected each other's talent and contribution to the film. She was absolutely delighted when her co-star won the Oscar blah, blah, blah. It could have been true but I doubt it.

However, she did express irritation at the way her role in *An Officer and a Gentleman* had been truncated in the cutting room which then made little sense of the subtleties of her performance. Most of all, she confessed to being one of the voices of *E.T.* in Steven Spielberg's hit movie. The voice had officially been accredited to another actress, Mercedes McCambridge, but when *E.T.* became ill and was dying, Spielberg used Debra's more husky voice.

The best screen Sherlock Holmes and Dr. Watson I met were Christopher Plummer and James Mason respectively when they were making *Murder by Decree*. Once again I was the interviewer. Both were experienced and spoke well. It was the third time I had met Mr. Plummer but did not remind him of that fact. Why should he remember? James Mason was by far the more likeable of the two. After the interview, he walked with me back to the set chatting comfortably all the way. Part of the plot involved Holmes and Watson's investigation of the slaying of prostitutes by Jack the Ripper. The French-Canadian actress, Genevieve Bujold, played one of his victims. She was not an easy interviewee, she was nervous and that made me nervous, but she did her best. After all, English is not her mother tongue. The Victorian sets were most realistic and on the day of my visit the setting was an asylum which I found disturbing.

When the premiere of *One Flew Over the Cuckoo's Nest* was held in London, its stars, Jack Nicholson and Louise Fletcher gave a press conference at the Dorchester Hotel. Also in attendance was the director, Milos Foreman, and the two producers Paul Zaentz and a young Michael Douglas. He was only 30, had just finished the successful TV series *The Streets of San Francisco* and was yet to make his mark as a movie actor. None was available for a TV interview so off I trotted, minus the other Barry, to get the low-down on what promised to be the year's hottest movie.

I caught up with Michael Douglas, now a film actor, only occasionally a producer, in New York in 1979 when he was publicising his latest film *The China Syndrome*. He and his co-stars Jane Fonda and Jack Lemmon were available to be interviewed for European TV. It was a very simple set-up and quite cost effective. I travelled alone to New York with three rolls of 16mm film stock. Each roll lasted 10 minutes. Other interviewers from Paris, Rome, Amsterdam and elsewhere did the same. The film company provided an American crew who were stationed in one room of a hired hotel suite in downtown Manhattan.

As each interviewer entered the room, they handed their roll of film to the cameraman to load into his camera. Each interview could then only last a maximum of ten minutes. The cameraman would then take the exposed roll of film from his camera and hand it to you, the interviewer, for processing. It was factory planning but it worked. I had the advantage of being from the BBC so was given the first interview slot.

Jane Fonda was the first of the trio. I had been told she would only talk about *The China Syndrome*, nothing else. This was a pity as I wanted to get a statement from her on the changing role of women in movies for a future edition of Barry Norman's weekly programme. She was well-groomed and charming, looked me straight in the eye as she spoke and gave me all she had. She is a bright, articulate woman and spoke eloquently about everything I asked. Now it was time for the kill. I posed the next question: *How does your role in The China Syndrome reflect the changing role of women in movies these days?* I got just the answer I needed for that future programme. I adored her. Moments later I impressed her, the cameraman and even myself when I uttered the usual final words *Jane Fonda, thank you*, thus finishing the interview just as the 400ft roll of film ran out. After years of working in TV I must have developed an inner time clock. I just *knew* when ten minutes had elapsed. Exactly the same thing happened at the end of my other interviews with Jack Lemmon and the above-mentioned Michael Douglas later the same afternoon. I was particularly sorry when I bade my farewell to the great Jane. I felt a bond that would make us friends for life. Ten minutes later I passed her in the hotel corridor. She walked straight past me as if she had never seen me in her life.

After the end of the Michael Douglas interview things were different. He held my maroon patterned tie, admired it and asked where I had bought it. *It was a birthday gift from my daughter,* I replied. Was he interested or was he just being polite? One never knows with actors. Jack Lemmon drank whisky to calm his nerves, spoke well then left.

The following week Barry Norman and two members of the production team joined me to record a New York edition of *Film 79*. The videotape would be then despatched by courier to London for transmission the next evening. Until this experience, I had been critical of BBC bureaucracy and its consequent inefficiency. Not any more. American movie companies were worse.

I worked on the programme from the BBC's New York office at the Rockefeller Center. Two blocks away were the offices of 20ᵗʰ Century Fox. I wanted stills and clips from their latest hit *Norma Rae* starring Sally Field. The publicist told me he was unable to provide them because he only covered domestic TV, that international TV was handled by their Los Angeles office. I insisted that I was making a programme in a New York studio about the week's movie offerings in the Big Apple. He would not budge. I rang 20ᵗʰ Century Fox International in LA and true to their word all the necessary material was on my desk first thing the next morning, having been sent 3000 miles by courier overnight. The identical material existed a few blocks away. The other distributors were little better. All large companies are inefficient - it is a fact of life.

The next day we went to film a story about the revived Astoria Studios at Queens, a New York suburb. I was looking forward to it because that was where the Marx Bros had made their film debut in *The Cocoanuts* in 1929. The well known director Sidney Lumet, a native New Yorker, had been a prime mover on the restoration project and was filming *Just Tell Me What You Want* with Ali MacGraw. Apart from the stars and director, I also met the British production designer, Tony Walton, Julie Andrews' first husband and father of Emma; also Jay Presson Allen who had adapted the screenplay from her novel. She had also adapted *Cabaret, The Prime of Miss Jean Brodie* and *Travels With My Aunt* for the screen. Until that day I had assumed that Jay Presson Allen was a man.

It was fascinating to see such an old building in operation once more but I feared for its future. Compared to British film studios, it was tiny and cramped with no room for expansion. The BBC New York office had a British film crew on secondment from London which we wanted to use. But in order to enter the studio with our three-man team, we had to pay also for an American cameraman, assistant, sound recordist, sound assistant and lighting technician, who did no work at all that day. Unions within the movie industry there were more constricting than they were in the UK.

It was now *Film 79* production day. The Astoria Studios story had been edited, all the still photographs to be used in the recording had been numbered and placed in order, the film clips had been spliced onto one roll for playing into the programme and Barry Norman's script had been typed on to the US equivalent of autocue. Rehearsal was due to begin. There was only one snag. I was to be the studio director and I had not done so for ten years. I found it was like riding a bike. Once you've done it you never forget.

Things went fairly well and after rehearsal we made a few minor adjustments, had a short lunch break, then it was time to record the programme in the HBO Studio at East 23rd St. Barry was determined not to fluff his lines, I was determined to direct everything calmly, according to the script, and Jill Talbot, my Producer's Assistant, was determined to cue in everything accurately. We recorded the whole ½ hour programme in one take without a hitch. At the end of recording the whole American studio crew burst into applause. It was fantastic. They said almost in unison *I didn't know you could make programmes this way.* They told us that other programmes were recorded in short bursts then edited together later at great expense. Not one of the technicians had even heard of the Astoria Studios so were fascinated by the 16mm location report and bemoaned the fact that American TV never bothered with such stories. It was a wonderful day.

Three years later I went on my own to Los Angeles on another 'junket' for European TV producers. It surprised me but three US film companies, Warner Bros, Universal and Polygram, had combined to finance a small team from European TV stations to cover their latest offerings. It was the one and only time it ever happened. Electronic Press Kits were just being devised. They contained on video, rather than on film, movie clips, interviews with the stars, location reports, still photographs on each movie and were distributed around the world by the movie moguls, thus negating the need for further expense by cash-strapped TV stations to send their own crews and interviewers to cover a movie. This also enabled the moguls to have more control over what was broadcast. Well, almost. It was OK for tiny stations to adapt this material for their local news programmes but they were often inadequate for the needs of specialist programme makers.

I was pleased to be one of the last to use this old tried and tested system which was almost identical to the New York experience with *The China Syndrome*. I took my rolls of 16mm film stock from London, handed them as required to the US cameraman, filmed each interview and took the exposed footage back to the UK for processing and editing. So after 6 days away from London , I returned with interviews of Dudley Moore, Mary Tyler Moore and the young ballerina Katherine Healey, who had all starred in *Six Weeks* directed by Tony Bill - yes, I also got to chat with him; Anthony Perkins who was making *Psycho II*; the actress Kathryn Harrold, whose claim to fame was appearing opposite Pavarotti in his only film role - er, flop *Yes, Gorgio* but had just made a rather good horror film called *The Sender;* and Ron Howard, teenage star of TV's *Happy Days* by now a movie director with *Night Shift* under his belt. Not a bad week.

Mary Tyler Moore disappointed me. I had loved her on TV, she had always reminded me of my ex-wife, and here I was, face to face with this warm-hearted, amusing, attractive woman from *The Mary Tyler Moore Show*. She was not warm at all. In fact, she was rather cold, more like the uptight mother she played in *Ordinary People*. She was lined and heavily made up. I could tell she was stressed. She was uninterested in me - her prime concern was how she was being 'lit'. When the camera started rolling her generous mouth opened into a wide smile and she was charming.

As soon as her performance was over she became cold and self-obsessed again.

Dudley Moore was warmer but also self-obsessed. I told him I had played his role in the Australian production of the hit British sixties stage review *Beyond the Fringe*. He was most unimpressed. Anthony Perkins was as weird as you would expect Norman Bates to be. It was a case of type casting. His saving grace was a wicked sense of humour. Although tall and somewhat gaunt, he was better looking off screen which is not always the case.

Kathryn Harrold was somewhat temperamental, that tell-tale sign of insecurity. Possibly that is why no-one remembers her anymore. The nicest interviewee of the lot was Ron Howard, the actor-turned-director. He was co-operative and unpretentious, wholly unconcerned about his receding hairline, more conscious of his desire to be a good movie director, which he has now become. *Parenthood* is one of my favourite movies.

The most rewarding afternoon's work took place at London's Savoy Hotel one Saturday afternoon in 1976 when MGM had gathered several Hollywood stars to tour Europe, promoting their compilation film sequel *That's Entertainment II*. Barry Norman turned up to interview Fred Astaire, Gene Kelly, Cyd Charisse, Donald O'Connor, Kathryn Grayson, Johnny Weissmuller, the music director Saul Chaplin, and the film's producer, Daniel Melnick. I have mentioned already my meetings with Tarzan and Kathryn Grayson so I shall concentrate on the others.

I had met Gene Kelly once before so I knew what to expect. In 1974 he came to London when the first *That's Entertainment* movie was premiered. After the Press Showing there was a buffet lunch for him at the swish Ivy Restaurant. I arrived a little late but had time for a brief chat with the producer/compiler Jack Haley Jnr. (his father was the Tin Man in *The Wizard of Oz*) and his then wife Liza Minnelli.

By the time I entered the restaurant itself everyone had helped themselves to the buffet and were eating at the surrounding tables. The central table was full of London showbiz journalists trading gossip, gulping down red wine and smoking profusely so I sat at a table at the side which was almost empty. The man next to me turned and said *Hi, I'm Gene Kelly.* I could not have engineered such an encounter. He talked about himself all the time but that is not a criticism, that is what I wanted to hear and he knew it. He was obviously very proud of *Invitation to the Dance* which was a flop at the box office and was pleased to have initiated and achieved a remarkable dance with the cartoon character Jerry of *Tom and Jerry* fame in *Anchors Aweigh.*

At the Savoy there was not much for me to do because Barry Norman was the interviewer and I had my colleague, Ann Freer, to direct. I just had to make sure everything went smoothly. If there was any animosity between Gene Kelly and Fred Astaire, as had been widely reported over the years, it was not apparent that weekend. They were aware of their differing dance styles but were respectful of each other's talent. And Fred wore the better hairpiece.

Although *That's Entertainment II* was a compilation of great moments from vintage MGM movies, the links between the sequences were sung and danced by Astaire and Kelly. The routines were not strenuous, Astaire was 77 and Kelly was 64, but they were a joy to watch. Before then the only time they had danced together was Gershwin's *The Babbitt and the Bromide* sequence in *Ziegfeld Follies* 30 years earlier. You could tell Fred Astaire had a more nervous and tense disposition than Gene Kelly, but both came across well in their interviews, neither saying anything revealing or contentious. None of the interviewees did that afternoon - they knew who was paying the bill at the end of the day. Nevertheless, I was thrilled at the signed photo I received of the two dance legends together.

Another screen dancer, Donald O'Connor whose *Make 'Em Laugh* sequence from *Singing' In The Rain* is a movie classic, was now overweight and had little to say. I sensed he had some kind of a chip on his shoulder about Hollywood but at the premiere the following evening, he left the usual red carpet when he saw me amongst the throng, came over and chatted. My companion that evening was most impressed.

Cyd Charisse was still slim and glamorous with big brown eyes, a generous mouth, a flattering hairstyle and long, long legs of which she was still proud at the age of 55. No matter how old, dancers always stand gracefully. Once my TV colleague, Ludovic Kennedy introduced me to his wife, Moira *(The Red Shoes)* Shearer, who, in turn, introduced me to the ageing ballerina Dame Alicia Markova. What I remember most about them was how straight and elegantly they stood at all times. My daughter, Amanda, was a professional dancer and even though she is now in her fifties, I am always aware of the way she stands too, with such poise.

Miss Charisse was no exception - she had changed her name from Tula Ellice Finklea. She seemed pre-occupied about finding the time during her short London stay to buy a suitable gift for her husband, Tony Martin the crooner, but being the true pro she is, she gave a good performance on camera.

The filming ended with an interesting interview with Saul Chaplin, the song writer, musical arranger and co-producer of *That's Entertainment II*. Then the UK representative of the film company offered me Fred Astaire's theatre tickets for that evening. The ageing Astaire did not want to see the hit show *Side by Side By Sondheim* featuring Millicent Martin, Julia McKenzie and David Kernan, with Ned Sherrin as narrator so off I went with a friend to the Mermaid Theatre to sit in fabulous seats for this fabulous show. At the interval, the woman sitting in front of me did not want to leave her seat, so she turned to chat to me instead. It was Cyd Charisse. I treasure that evening at the theatre.

When the edited item was transmitted about *That's Entertainment II,* featuring those interviews with that galaxy of stars and interspersed with some great clips from their movies, it was quite unexciting. I was unaware of its lack of impact until I saw the programme at home in my own living room. That is one of the perils of being a TV producer. An incredible personal experience does not always result in an incredible experience on-screen. Sometimes you cannot see the wood for the trees.

The most exciting overseas filming trip Barry and I had was in January 1979 when we flew with a party of European journalists and TV interviewers to Rio de Janeiro to cover the making of the James Bond film *Moonraker.* It was basically a simple story about how Bond sets out to investigate the disappearance of a space shuttle during a test flight. His adventures had taken him to Venice and Paris but we were concentrating on that section of the plot in Rio at carnival time, which included a dangerous encounter on a cable car on Sugar Loaf Mountain.

After our long flight via Frankfurt, we checked in to the Meridien Hotel right on Copocabana Beach and early next morning attended a hastily assembled meeting. The publicist announced that, owing to a painful kidney stone, Roger Moore was still in Paris. However, James Bond's leading lady, Lois Chiles, would be available for interviews during the day. The BBC back in London would be really pleased - they fly the pair of us to Rio to cover a James Bond movie and return without any footage of the man himself, just his co-star, a little-known actress.

However, that evening things livened up and we forgot our misfortune when the hotel gave a party for their European guests and performed a mini-version of the Rio Carnival in its spacious ballroom. The previous year's Carnival procession was being reassembled for the movie anyway as the real one was more than a month away. After many samplings of South American booze I felt quite uninhibited and willingly joined the tall, dark, near-naked, feather-costumed ladies on the dance floor when they beckoned. As the hypnotic South American music became louder and faster, I started high kicking from side to side with my arms around my female companions, trying to compete with them. I was dressed head to toe in white, I remember - very tropical. The other Barry was astonished at my brazenness.

On the second day in Rio de Janeiro, we assembled at the base of Sugar Loaf Mountain to board a cable car to the top. There we would film a spectacular stunt shot of a fight in the cable car as it travelled across the ravine. Before we left the movie publicist made a solemn announcement in his strong American accent.

Ladies and gentlemen, I am pleased to report that at 6.17am Paris time Roger Moore successfully passed his kidney stone. He will be flying immediately on Concorde to commence filming in Rio de Janeiro.

He expected a round of applause, all he got from me was a secret sigh of relief. The view from Sugar Loaf Mountain was spectacular. Both Barry and I have difficulty with heights but we did our best to disguise our fear as we watched the filming.

Next afternoon, back in town, Barry and I walked along the promenade of Copacabana Beach surely one of the sexiest places in the world where beautiful women and men, wearing next to nothing, bask on the beach, swim in the surf or play volleyball on the white sand. The ethnic mix of South America has provided Brazil with a race of astonishingly sexy people. This was heaven.

Suddenly an open-topped car came spinning round the corner with Roger Moore inside. Another car with camera attached, filmed alongside. Most people on the street did not even realise James Bond was in their midst. Shortly afterwards Roger was being driven back to his hotel after the filming sequence, when he recognised Barry Norman. He shouted out to both of us. *Come to dinner at the Copacabana Palace Hotel, Presidential Suite at 8 o'clock.* We gave him the thumbs up.

And so it came to pass that as I was having a martini, prepared by James Bond with his wife Luisa and the other Barry seated alongside, Roger Moore showed me the jagged kidney stone he had passed earlier in Paris. No wonder he had been in agony, it was enormous. It seemed like a bizarre dream. We then went to the hotel dining room for dinner where we were joined by the director Lewis Gilbert and his wife Hilda. I have no recollection of what I ate but it was a jovial meal and our table was the centre of attention the whole evening. It was rather unnerving.

We returned to Sugar Loaf Mountain the next day to film the promised interview with Roger Moore. There were two film crews waiting, one for the European TV teams the other for the Latin Americans. Roger gave his usual performance on camera. He is quite endearing and always self-deprecating. It is his defence mechanism for not having to reveal anything he does not wish you to know.

Roger was summoned to another part of the mountain to do an interview with the Latin American crew. He returned 15 minutes later saying *you won't believe this. I've just finished the interview and now the Brazilian cameraman tells me he forgot to put film in the camera.* I did not want to reveal my secret about French filters! It turned out to be a genuine mistake and Roger obligingly returned to be interviewed all over again.

Years later Roger came to the BBC studios one Bank Holiday Monday to record an interview with Barry Norman for the following week's programme. It was about his role in his final Bond film *A View To A Kill*. Afterwards I escorted him from the studio to his waiting car outside TV Centre. Because of the holiday, fewer members of staff were wandering the corridors so I thought it would be a simple journey. No way. How does word get around that someone famous is in the building? I had only alerted the receptionist. People emerged from nooks and crannies in the building asking for his autograph. There must have been twenty all told during that short journey. He obliged them all. *Don't you get tired of all this?* I enquired sympathetically. *No,* he replied and bade farewell.

Seventeen

The Man
With No Name

Apart from a phone call to the *Film Night* office in 1968, I had never had any contact with Clint Eastwood. I had seen him on TV as *Rawhide* and admired his lanky frame and natural good looks. I saw those Spaghetti Westerns he made in Italy with Sergio Leone in which his enigmatic persona as *The Man With No Name* worked a treat. I could not believe he had been dropped by Universal Studios. I never saw his first film role as a laboratory assistant in *The Revenge of the Creature* until it became part of a career compilation for his American Film Institute's Life Achievement Award in 1996.

Over the years I had shown clips on the programme of Clint in *Coogan's Bluff* when he played a lawman from Arizona who goes to New York to show the cops there how to track down a wanted man; I enjoyed his natural singing voice and his laconic acting style in the movie version of the Lerner and Loew musical *Paint Your Wagon*; I admired his directorial debut in *Play Misty For Me* and the perfect mood he created when he, as a late night radio DJ, was stalked by a psychotic fan; I liked his sense of comedy in *Thunderbolt and Lightfoot* when as an escaped bank robber he impersonated a preacher and befriended drifter Jeff Bridges; I enjoyed his catchphrase *make my day* in the *Dirty Harry* movies; and although I found the violence disturbing in *The Outlaw Josey Wales,* I could see how well he handled the action sequences in this epic Western.

By now Clint had formed his own production company, Malpaso, on the Warner Bros lot in Burbank and had a busy life as producer, director and star. He had never been interviewed on British TV until my colleague, Iain Johnstone, made a documentary about him for BBC TV in 1976 as part of America's Bicentenary Celebrations. It was a huge success.

Out of the blue Barry Norman and I received an invitation the following year to interview Clint Eastwood in New York for the opening of his latest film *The Gauntlet* in which he was both star and director. It was my first trip to the Big Apple. Barry showed me Barnes and Noble bookstore and commented that *no place can be all that bad with bookstores like this.* Barry was addicted to bookstores. The core of Barry's life is words and he expresses his love of them in his movie reviews. It is what he says and the way he says it that are as important as the movies he is reviewing. His loyal viewers watched him for the wonderful words he chose- sometimes, funny, sometimes poignant, usually relevant and always succinct.

When we visited that bookstore we were on our way to a screening of Clint's latest film. He played a disreputable cop, his co-star, Sondra Locke, played a prostitute. Wait a minute. Sondra Locke. Wasn't she also his co-star in *The Outlaw Josey Wales?* I had seen her wondrous performance in Carson McCullers' *The Heart Is A Lonely Hunter* way back in 1968. I don't know when the penny dropped, but it became apparent that Clint was having an affair with Sondra and that by making himself more available for TV interviews he could travel legitimately to New York to be with his mistress, while his wife Maggie and kids Kyle and Alison stayed home in Carmel, California. Was this the reason for his sudden accessibility?

Because of jet lag I dozed during the screening but still recall the movie's wonderful jazz score. The other Barry, being the true professional, saw it all.

The big interview with the great Clint Eastwood took place the following morning in a suite at Drake's Hotel where we were staying. He is an impressive man - 6'4" with a big, lean, frame, a quiet, laid-back manner and an enigmatic smile, and he is only 4 months younger than me! He and Barry Norman got on well so the interview went smoothly and easily and I was thrilled at the prospect of editing and showing it on *Film 77.*

I have mentioned elsewhere about how an interview was filmed on 16mm in those days before video became the norm. Suffice to remind you that, as only one camera was available, the interview was shot over Barry Norman's shoulder, facing the star. On each question the cameraman would slowly zoom in or out to change the size of the shot, sometimes medium shot, sometimes wide shot, usually close-up.

In normal circumstances, the busy star usually leaves the premises immediately after the main interview and I, as stand-in, sit in the star's position while Barry's questions are filmed all over again. When edited together, the impression is given that there were two cameras filming both star and interviewer. Sometimes if an actor or actress seems sympathetic to your needs, you ask them if you could film one 2-shot of actor and interviewer together from a different angle. Clint seemed that sort of guy and sure enough he agreed to my suggestion. The shot was filmed. Then Clint asked me if there was anything more we needed from him. He was happy to stay so we filmed some more. As a movie director as well as actor, he was aware of these technicalities - in fact, he was intrigued by them.

We shot every possible combination of Clint and Barry and I no longer needed him to stay. Not that I said so. He still hovered and looked at the Arriflex camera being used and the Nagra tape recorder. Then he looked at me and felt the lapel of my jacket. It was made of brown Donegal tweed. *That's a lovely suit you're wearing,* he remarked, *where did you get it?*

My reply was wholly truthful, *£20 at a closing-down Sale in Golders Green.*

Eventually it was I who had to beg Clint to excuse us as we had a plane to catch to London. He then shook hands with everyone and thanked *us* for the interview. It should have been the other way round. We had bonded well. Fancy having to tell Clint Eastwood to leave!

The following year the other Barry and I flew to Dallas where Clint had invited us to attend the world premiere of his latest film *Every Which Way But Loose.* His co-star was Clyde, an orang-utan. After the screening the movie company gave all who had attended an inscribed bomber jacket stating the name of the film, its location and date of the screening. I wore it proudly for years but eventually donated it to my local charity shop.

That evening we were taken to an out-of-town site, so prevalent in the USA, to a luxurious theatre restaurant. The food was southern fried chicken, corn on the cob, all finger-lickin' good. I drank my first ever pino colada, liked the mixture of pineapple juice and coconut forgetting it was laced with rum, had a second and a third. And I froze. Why is air conditioning in the USA so strong? We sat in a huge semi-circle of tiered rows of dark blue comfy seats with tables in front and watched the floor show. If I had been a Country & Western fan I would have been thrilled at the line-up of stars but I did not know any of them. There was an older guy with a pony tail called Willie Nelson and a younger, dark-haired singer by the strange name of Eddie

Rabbitt. Clint made a brief appearance but did not sing. He's a ballad man, or so I thought. How was I to know that he was about to play a country singer in a later movie?

The next day we interviewed Clint Eastwood. This time Sondra Locke hovered although the star did not introduce her to us. All I remember was that she was overly made up. She was in the movie too but there was no way Clint would allow her to be interviewed by us. During the filming of his chat with the other Barry, Clint was as laid-back as ever. If he needs time to think he does so. No-one minds, except me, the producer. I want all interviews on the programme to have pace and wit to keep the late-night audience awake. His natural pace is laconic and he is full of charm - not the boy next door but the man who knows best.

At the end of the interview Clint took a publicity photograph of him with Clyde the orang-utan and autographed it for me. When he handed it back, I could tell by the way he looked that he wanted me to read it and enjoy the joke. I did just that and provided him with a forced chuckle. The truth is I could not read his handwriting. Only when packing my bag to return to London did I decipher it: *To Barry. How about the co-star? Best Wishes, Clint.*

The following year I attended the Deauville Film Festival. The arrangement was that Barry Norman and I would have breakfast with Clint at his hotel, before filming the interview in the garden. We had already seen his new movie *Broncho Billy* which would give Clint plenty to talk about. It was a definite change of direction for him and he gave a remarkably low-key performance as a would-be cowboy from New Jersey. Clint was the director as well. If Sondra Locke accompanied him on this trip, she did not join us for breakfast.

Clint was a little late. He had been up early to visit the nearby sites of the Normandy landings during World War II which fascinated him. We, the two Barrys, ordered the usual

Contintental breakfast on offer, as one is apt to do in France. Not Clint. He quietly excused himself, wandered into the kitchen and had a chat with the chef. Several minutes later out came the eggs, just as Clint wanted them. How's that for manipulation? I can imagine the surprise on the chef's face when a tall, lanky, film star dressed in a white T- Shirt and jeans turned out to be Dirty Harry.

In January 1983 Clint made a quick trip to London, en route from Paris where he had received some prestigious French award. His distributors, Warner Bros, decided to arrange a last-minute dinner in his honour at the Arts Club in Dover St. It was a Sunday evening, my 53rd birthday and very cold. My son Dugald was living with me at the time so he was my guest. How many would turn up to such a hastily arranged function? As it happened, just about everyone.

My son gawped as Dudley Moore walked by, followed by a shambling Walter Matthau with his eccentric wife in deathly white make-up. A little later, a tall, elegant woman arrived and I knew she shared my birthday. When I called out *Happy Birthday,* she came over. I told her it was my birthday too - ages were not discussed although *The Sunday Times* that morning mentioned that she was 42. She gave me a great big kiss. I did not remind her that I had met her once before when she had been to BBC TV Centre to be interviewed about playing Joan Crawford in *Mommie Dearest.*

When she had left to join her husband, my son enquired politely *who the hell is that?* He had not recognised Faye Dunaway.

It reminded me of the time 25 years earlier when Jane Russell arrived at the ABC Studios in Sydney to be interviewed. I was bitterly disappointed; she looked nothing like the Jane Russell I had seen in *The Outlaw* and *Gentlemen Prefer Blondes.* But when she was in the studio itself, in front of the cameras, miraculously she became the Jane Russell I had known of yore. Faye Dunaway was the same. The camera liked her.

The dinner began and Dugald and I were seated far away from the main table where Clint was guest of honour. I wanted to renew my acquaintance with the star but it was not to be. Seated beside me was Dilys Powell, the noted British film critic, now well into her eighties and still working. She was worried, as people of that age do, whether she would have any success hailing a taxi home in such appalling weather. To allay her fears I offered to drive her home whenever she was ready to leave. Unfortunately, she wanted to go sooner than Dugald and I would have wished, so there was no way I could get the chance to speak again to Clint. Dilys was most grateful for the lift home.

Later I learned two things. Unbeknown to me, she had been escorted to the top table earlier in the evening to meet the man himself, as the doyen of British critics. Also Dudley Moore and Clint Eastwood had played jazz duets on the piano well into the early hours of the morning. It turned out to be a raucous evening.

Subsequently I have followed Clint's career with more than a passing interest and was delighted when he eventually won Best Picture and Best Director Oscars for his 1992 Western *Unforgiven* and again in 2005 for *Million Dollar Baby*. I was overjoyed when he was recognised by the American Film Institute and honoured in 1996 with their Life Achievement Award. This event made me realise what a maverick he is.

In the audience were the usual crowd, Dustin Hoffman, Warren Beatty, Gregory Peck, Jack Nicholson, but the show was hosted by Jim Carrey, who had appeared with him seven years earlier in *Pink Cadillac;* and by Rene Russo, his co-star in the more recent *In the Line of Fire*. Those who paid tribute were not the starry line-up usually associated with this kind of ceremony. They were Jessica Walter, Geoffrey Lewis, Forrest Whitaker, Jeff Fahey, Gary Busey, Mario van

Peebles and Quincy Jones. The Life Achievement Award, a stunning piece of sculpture which I am sure will not rust a la Manila style, was presented to Clint by the only major 'name' of the evening, the previous year's recipient Steven Spielberg who likened Clint's laid-back style of movie-making to his lifelong love of jazz. In fact, the highlight of the evening was Clint's son Kyle, now a well known jazz bass player, playing extremely well for his Dad.

The clips which illustrated the tribute showed what a fine actor and director Clint Eastwood had become. Clint himself made a rambling, unprepared response, saying how overwhelming it was to see his career flash before his eyes and other such platitudes. His laconic style made him a bad speechmaker. No good for weddings and not much better for Life Achievement Awards. It was good to see his proud mother beaming beside him at the main table as well as his new wife, Dina Ruiz but first wife Maggie and Sondra Locke did not get a mention.

I eventually worked out that Clint Eastwood has fathered 7 children from 5 different women. But that's not why he has kept on working - he simply enjoys what he does. These days he even composes his own film scores. His mother lived to 97. I think Clint is aiming to do the same.

Eighteen   The Hollywood Greats

Noel Coward once said that television was for appearing on. I say that television is better to work in than to watch. I came to this conclusion when I saw on BBC1 in 1977 the first series of 5 x 50 minute documentaries I had produced called *The Hollywood Greats.* I just loved working on them. They were also popular with viewers and they were shown in a prime time slot, the hour preceding the *Nine O' Clock News.* Don't get me wrong, I was proud of the series but no programme you make is ever perfect and insignificant glitches become glaringly noticeable during actual transmission. Although I found working on *The Hollywood Greats* a joy, it was also a nightmare. Yet it was far more exciting and demanding than any viewer could imagine. Much heartache and debate is endured by all concerned - it is par for the course. The premise I eventually adopted for the series was to reveal *the person behind the screen image;* but to begin with, the production team and I did not know what kind of documentaries we were going to make.

It all started towards the end of 1976 when Bryan Cowgill, still Controller BBC1, contacted my Head of Department saying that he wanted Barry Norman to present five documentaries during July/August 1977. He needed them for his summer schedule. The irony is that it was harder to churn out a ½ hour film programme week after week than to produce a five-part 50- minute documentary series. Everyone in TV takes a weekly programme for granted but when you produce something special and it is a critical and viewing success, you become a well-known name in the industry. Cowgill was pleased with Barry Norman's progress as a national TV host and wanted to feature him more prominently the following year. This would deflect press and viewer criticism that much of the BBC1 schedule during 'the silly season' comprised 'repeats'.

A series of discussions about what kind of documentary series to make eventually led us to *All Time Cinema Greats*. It would combine 'dead' movie star profiles like Clark Gable and Humphrey Bogart with others who were still very much alive, like Fred Astaire, Katharine Hepburn and Robert Mitchum. The criterion was that without any doubt they could be considered 'cinema greats'. Research into several lives began and I started writing letters:

Room 7000A   BBC TV Centre,
Wood Lane London W12 7RJ

7 December 1976
Mr. Fred Astaire
c/o "The Purple Taxi"
Ardmore Studios   IRELAND

Dear Fred Astaire,

You may remember we met at the Savoy Hotel in May this year when Barry Norman, the presenter/interviewer of FILM 76, the programme I produce, filmed an interview with you and Gene Kelly for a special edition of the programme devoted to "That's Entertainment Part II".

We did not have the time-slot to allow us to use all the good material contained in that interview, and this has given rise to a new project with Barry Norman called "ALL TIME CINEMA GREATS, a series of 5 x 50 minute documentaries for screening on BBC1 next July in a prime time slot, 8pm.

Naturally, we would like very much to devote one of these documentaries to you. The programme would be thoroughly researched and made with care and affection by an informed and professional production team. It would also contain a selection of relevant feature film extracts plus other interviews with your friends and colleagues and, hopefully, your daughter Ava and sister Adele.

However, if we obtain your permission to make this documentary (and I have my fingers crossed that you will agree) we would need a further filmed conversation by Barry Norman with you alone, as well as some random location shots of you at work in Ireland on "The Purple Taxi".

This would only involve a couple of hours of interview filming off set, say a morning or afternoon, in Ireland at a time and place convenient to you. I assure you it could all be done in a relaxed and pleasant manner.

No doubt at this stage in the filming of "The Purple Taxi" you have had more than your share of newspaper interviews already, but we in Britain would be so delighted to have a filmed documentary record of your illustrious career, that I ask you, most sincerely, to give some serious consideration to this request.

The bearer of this letter, Mr. Fred Hift, will vouch for the production team's credentials, and Mr. Alan Warner of United Artists Records, with whom you worked so closely on your last LP, also knows of our professional approach to this kind of cinema programme.

We would be honoured if you would consent to be one of our "ALL TIME CINEMA GREATS".

Yours sincerely
BARRY BROWN
Producer, Film Programmes Unit

We all waited for his reply. It arrived in his handwriting with my original letter attached.

Royal Hibernian Hotel
Dawson St
DUBLIN 2
Wed. Dec 15

Dear Barry Brown

I am not available for this "Cinema Greats" program mentioned in the enclosed letter which was just handed to me. I am not interested in the project <u>at any price</u> and will not be a participant. I have much important work to do in this film and do not want to be bothered in the least with anything else. Final.

Very truly yours
F. Astaire

That was telling me. After all he was 77 at the time. It is a pity *The Purple Taxi*, his final movie, turned out to be so awful with Fred Astaire miscast as the eccentric Irish doctor.

At the same time, we were being given the run around in Los Angeles by Robert Mitchum's agent. After my experience with the actor on *Ryan's Daughter* I was reluctant to include him in the series but he was definitely an *All Time Cinema Great*. Each time one of my co-producers Judy Lindsay telephoned, her hopes were raised because he had not rejected the proposal but was still considering it. I should have known better. This was 'Hollywood speak' for letting her down gently.

By late January, Mitchum was still considering. Filming had to begin in April, because the editing had to begin in May if all 5 documentaries were to be ready for transmission in July. This also meant that Judy Lindsay needed to be in Los Angeles by mid-March to finalise interviews and locations. Before she left she would have to prepare 5 research documents on each 'cinema great', so that relevant movie clips could be collated for inclusion in each programme. Time was running out.

On the last Friday in January I came into the office and made my decisive speech to the assembled production team, who, remember, were still making the weekly *Film 77* programme. We would have to forget about movie stars who were still alive. We must choose 5 dead movie stars, all men, and all from the same period in Hollywood history, as if it had always been our intention to do so. It would be called *The Hollywood Greats*. By the end of the day we had our chosen five - Clark Gable, Errol Flynn, Spencer Tracy, Gary Cooper and Humphrey Bogart. It is amazing what is born out of necessity. It was the best decision of my career. I learned that it is only when people are deceased will others tell the truth. However, there were some disappointments. Katharine Hepburn refused to talk about Spencer Tracy and at the last minute, Mary Astor was too ill to be interviewed about Humphrey Bogart and *The Maltese Falcon*.

Production plans intensified and filming began on time in April. I would direct and supervise the editing on Clark Gable and Humphrey Bogart, my colleague Margaret Sharp would be in charge of Errol Flynn and Gary Cooper and Judy Lindsay would do the same for Spencer Tracy. But a pact had to be made. If necessary, we had to film each other's interviews if that were the more practicable solution. Therefore, although I included Robert Wagner in my Gable documentary, I did not go to his two-storey house in Beverly Hills where he lived with his wife Natalie Wood whom he had recently remarried. Judy went because he also spoke about Spencer Tracy. And so it went on. We were just like factory workers on a production line. There are times when co-operation among producers is essential. For *The Hollywood Greats* it was vital.

The team comprised a BBC cameraman and his assistant, sound recordist, electrician, myself, two other producer/directors, a producer's assistant and Barry Norman. We filmed everything in 4 weeks, apart from a few interviews later in London and Paris. Many interviewees were only too pleased to co-operate because they had admired BBC programmes then showing on US Public Television. Over and over again I was told that the BBC series they enjoyed the most was *Upstairs, Downstairs.* I smiled, accepting their praise and acknowledging how grateful I was that they were willing to participate so readily because of this excellent TV series. I never once admitted it was made by London Weekend Television not the BBC!

To keep costs down we took advantage of Super Apex air fares so no flights could be altered. For the same reasons we were all booked into what turned out to be a rather sleazy motel on Sunset Boulevard near Tower Records. Barry Norman based his later novel *Have A Nice Day* on his experiences there. We soon realised that most of the motel's female guests worked day and night, mostly the latter, so we often saw sheepish gentlemen lurking in the corridors. We stayed at that motel for three consecutive years and things did not improve. I remember asking the other Barry whether he had seen a man staying there covered in bandages. He said he had not. He had seen a woman covered in bandages. Then we saw several people covered in bandages minding their own business. We learned later that a local plastic surgeon had booked his clients into the same motel so that he could monitor their post-operative progress. Only in California would such a bizarre situation arise.

Although we in the BBC team were like a family during our Californian sojourn, we never met for breakfast. I would wander each morning up to Ben Franks' 24 hour diner, sit on a stool at the counter and order my juice, bacon, eggs any way I liked and toast (white, wholemeal or rye). On the first morning there, I knew how I wanted my eggs cooked. When asked, I said *over and out* mistakenly using aircraft jargon. I should have said *over easy*. From then on I ordered them *sunny side up,* which I preferred anyway.

The first morning's filming was a disaster. Here was my big opportunity, I had never made a 50' documentary before, let alone a whole series, and it was all going wrong. We drove to the home of one Clark Gable's production colleagues, Cornwall Jackson. He was a terrible interviewee. In every answer he made a snide reference to his ex-wife, the former screen actress, Gail Patrick, by now the producer of the successful TV series *Perry Mason.* He resented her success. We did not use one frame of this man's contribution in the edited documentary.

From then it could only get better and it did. The interview with director Mervyn Leroy who took credit for discovering *Clark Gable, that guy with the jug ears* was more memorable to me for another reason - his sumptuous office. He had no real work to do. He had been preparing the same movie project for 12 years. I got the impression that his wife wanted him out of the house so he went to an office block on Sunset Boulevard to talk to people like us and watch the odd baseball game in his viewing room.

I chatted to him at his office desk while the camera crew set up their equipment. That was part of my job. The other Barry hovered in the background preparing his questions for the actual filming. On the table behind me I suddenly recognised Dorothy's red shoes from *The Wizard of Oz.* I wanted to steal them. Leroy had been the producer of that classic movie. But what he revealed about Gable comprised only two short sentences in the transmitted documentary.

The next day I met Jean Garceau, secretary to both Gable and his wife Carole Lombard before the latter was killed in a plane crash in 1942 whilst selling war bonds. Her description of Clark on hearing of his wife's death was incredibly poignant. She also explained how the Hollywood star used the studio's craftsmen to carry out all his home repairs - carpenters, electricians, painters, you name them.

At producer Z. Wayne Griffin's office in downtown Los Angeles he recalled an instance when Gable for a joke on location, emerged from his tent without his false teeth. Not a pretty picture of a man dubbed *The King of Hollywood*. After filming this interview, Griffin told us about the magnificent views from the rooftop of the skyscraper. Up we went with the camera crew to get those general shots of Hollywood which you can easily forget to film, then need desperately in the cutting room when you are editing back in London. It is nondescript filler material but it comes in handy. The cameraman filmed Los Angeles traffic flowing on the freeway with the 'Hollywood' destination clearly marked on an overhead road sign; the Hollywood sign itself; the hills beyond - that kind of thing.

We went to Palm Springs and there I filmed two great Hollywood directors. At Rancho Mirage, Frank Capra, who had directed Gable in *It Happened One Night,* told us that unwittingly he and Gable had set the American trend of not wearing a vest under a shirt, simply because it would have spoiled the famous bedroom scene - it would have taken Gable too long to undress. Capra instructed Gable to *forget the vest.* US underwear manufacturers were livid. Sales plummeted once the movie had been released.

On the outskirts of this fabled town lived Howard Hawks the man who became famous for casting nineteen-year-old model Lauren Bacall opposite Humphrey Bogart in *To Have And Have Not.* He had also directed one of my favourite films *Bringing Up Baby.* When I phoned him the previous night he was quite cantankerous. I was not looking forward to filming him. When I and the crew turned up the next morning he was, in truth, pleased to see us. He was a lonely, forgotten man and enjoyed the attention we accorded him. He did not say much with that gravel voice of his, but when he did it was pertinent and apt. As an aside he told us he only filled the swimming pool for the dog to use. I noticed that his teenage son lay on a sofa and watched TV the whole time we were there. His housekeeper worked slowly in the desert heat but did not offer us a cold drink.

Because Howard Hawks had directed three of our five *Hollywood Greats,* Gable, Cooper and Bogart, Barry Norman interviewed him about all three. When he was asked three times in three separate interviews what special quality each of these actors had, he gave the one simple reply. *The camera liked him,* he growled. That was it in a nutshell.

Back in Los Angeles, the director George Cukor had a magnificent house north of St. Vincente Boulevard. The rooms were so tastefully decorated that you felt nobody ever went into them. The garden was one of the best I had ever seen, full of European and tropical shrubs in perfect splendour. He told me everything had been planted in the 1930s and left there. It was now mature, somewhat rare in Hollywood. At Cukor's house I sat by the swimming pool where Errol Flynn wooed his first wife Lily Damita, and where Hepburn and Tracy had conducted their discreet affair in the nearby guest lodge. Cukor now lived alone but had a valet. We were at his house for 3½ hours that morning and although we could smell a delicious meal being cooked in the nearby kitchen by his henchman, not once were we offered even a drink of water. It had nothing to do with meanness, only thoughtlessness, the by-product of a colossal ego. It was worse at the house of the egotistical Hollywood screenwriter, Leonard Spigelgass. While we were filming him he sipped tea and ate biscuits in front of us without batting an eyelid.

It was all very different at actress Virginia Grey's modest apartment in the San Fernando Valley. Her career had not flourished. She was a 60 year old, dark blonde beauty with high cheekbones, grey eyes and a gravel voice. She was very honest about her relationship with Gable, probably the wife he should have had. They had met when they were appearing together in *Test Pilot* in 1938 when she was just 21. She loved him a lot and it hurt. It was still there in her sad eyes. After the interview she announced, *gentlemen, the bar is yours*. It was a spontaneous gesture of generosity which was second nature to her and contrasted enormously with the behaviour of the mega-rich in more salubrious quarters.

We drove to La Jolla, a beach town just north of San Diego to receive comparable hospitality from writer/director Delmer Daves and his wife. He had been a friend of Gary Cooper and had written and directed Bogart in *Dark Passage* thirty years earlier. We focused the interview on these two actors although he knew just about everybody in the business. His wife had even more friends. When I told her of my difficulties in contacting certain stars for the series, she invited me to her bedroom.

There we sat on an unmade bed at 4 o'clock in the afternoon while she flicked through her address book. Under 'G' I saw written *Gable, Mrs. Clark* and a telephone number. She dialled it and learned that the star's widow was out of town for the next six weeks, so that put paid to an interview with her. I told Mrs. Daves that I was also looking for a cowboy star to reminisce about Gary Cooper, either Randolph Scott or Joel McCrea, neither of whom the production team had been able to contact. She thumbed through her book of contacts. I shall always treasure overhearing her chat with Randolph Scott.

Hi Randy. I haven't seen you since church on Christmas Eve. The BBC from England want to film an interview with you about Gary Cooper…. Yes… uh-huh…. oh….I see…yes, I understand………
Bye, Randy.

At least she tried. Later she turned to me and said *I know why Randolph Scott won't do that interview, he's deaf.* Using that joke Rita Tushingham had played on me in Tehran, I said *Pardon?* It was most inappropriate.

The next morning at my motel Joel McCrea rang me. He said he was too old to be filmed, he did not want people to see him as he looked now, but he was happy to do an audio interview. I rejected the offer politely but, thanks to Mrs. Daves, I did get that call. Before we left their wonderful house overlooking the Pacific Ocean I was persuaded to stay with them the next time I came to California. I would have loved that. Daves had been a writer at MGM for ten years until 1943 when he moved to Warner Bros. and added producing and directing to his bow. I could have talked to him for hours about old Hollywood. Alas, six weeks later, Delmer Daves was dead.

The original series of five *The Hollywood Greats* was a great success and so we made two more popular series. In 1978 I remained in London during filming because days before I was due to leave, I contracted hepatitis. However, weeks later in London, I was well enough to edit the Jean Harlow documentary and supervise the other four - Joan Crawford, Ronald Colman, Judy Garland and Charles Laughton. Another director, Sue Mallinson, joined the team and she wrote to me regularly with all the gossip. It cheered me up no end. The Crawford documentary was made before her adoptive daughter Christina had published *Mommie Dearest,* which denounced the star as a harsh and uncaring mother.

Whilst my colleagues were filming interviews with those who knew the star, Joan Crawford's stern treatment of her children emerged anyway. After the broadcast, the British press criticised the programme rather hysterically for demeaning the stature of one of Hollywood's greatest stars. Yet the following year they published extracts from *Mommie Dearest* without compunction. Not long after the broadcast, the movie producer, Herman Cohen, called me on another matter and took me to task over Barry Norman's treatment of the star. He had produced Miss Crawford's final film *Trog* in England. I began to apologise. *No,* he interrupted, *you weren't harsh enough!* In that documentary the comment I remember best came from actor Cliff Robertson who had starred with her in *Autumn Leaves*. He said *she could cry with either eye, on cue.* That is really something.

The final series of five documentaries in 1979 featured Charlie Chaplin, Groucho Marx, Edward G. Robinson, Marilyn Monroe and a general look at Hollywood during its 'golden years'. Barry Norman has written extensively about the content of these programmes in his two books *The Hollywood Greats* and *The Movie Greats*. So I shall continue with my reminiscences about the making of them.

I was glad to meet Zeppo Marx, the serious one in the Marx Bros. movies. By now he was the only survivor. He was more handsome than the others and looked extremely fit, like most retired actors who play golf regularly. Off camera, at every opportunity he would be disparaging about Frank Sinatra. I wondered why he needed to be so vitriolic. Then the penny dropped. His wife Barbara Marx had run off with the singer a couple of years earlier. In his younger days Zeppo had been a renowned womaniser. He could not cope when the tables were turned. I was surprised to read several months later that Zeppo had died of cancer. He had looked so well.

The hoofer who ended up in gangster pictures was George Raft. When I met him at his apartment in Century City he was dressed in a maroon silk dressing gown with a 'GR' monogram. He changed into his well-pressed suit only minutes before the filmed interview began. He was dapper. He was not a bright man; he confessed that he only read the sports pages of his daily newspaper. But he was full of charm in a New York gangsterish way.

This was the first time I had seen plastic flowers in someone's apartment. They were yellow and looked quite realistic, particularly when I saw tiny plastic petals on the table beside the vase! After the interview he took me into his bedroom. He jokingly told me he was fond of modern art and showed me an avant-garde picture above his king-sized bed. He told me to study it carefully. I did and eventually the F-word emerged from its myriad design. He laughed uproariously.

I was glad to meet Charlie Chaplin's second wife, Lita Grey Chaplin and the mother of two of his sons, Charles Jnr. and Sydney. She called herself Chaplin even though she had married again. That name meant something to her in Hollywood. Or did it? She worked as a saleslady at Robinson's department store in Beverly Hills and had taken the day off to earn her $1000 fee for the interview.

She lived quite modestly in a small apartment building in Fountain Avenue between Sunset and Santa Monica Boulevards. I found her charming and out-going and still most attractive with her greying black hair and big dark brown eyes. Chaplin was thirty-five when he had married her, Lita Grey was only sixteen. She had appeared as a twelve-year-old in Chaplin's movie *The Kid*. He put her under contract and wanted to star her in *The Gold Rush* but she became pregnant instead with Charles Jnr. who was born officially on 28 June 1925. In fact, Chaplin had bribed an official to change the real date, 5 May, to make it appear that the child had been conceived after marriage. By the time Chaplin had been forced to marry her, his ardour had cooled considerably but she bore him another son Sydney the following year.

Although the marriage was brief, Lita Grey, fifty years later, was able to give a dispassionate view of their relationship. He was enormously insecure. Even in restaurants, waiters intimidated him. He never felt that anyone loved him. Yet in his day he was the most famous man in the world. And his movies, which he wrote, produced, directed and starred in, earned him millions.

I remember taking the film crew to one of Chaplin's former homes near Griffith Park to get an exterior shot from the road. I had not sought permission from the current owner, not for such a brief shot. When we got there, all that was visible from the road was the mail box with the street number emblazoned on it. I sneaked up the driveway with the cameraman, hoping we would not be spotted. Officially we were trespassers, but I had to take the risk after all the trouble we had taken to find the place. Once the hand-held camera started rolling, dogs barked and a woman looked up from the kitchen where she was working. She was a Mexican maid. We got our shot, but only just.

Another memorable house we visited was the one in Brentwood occupied by Marilyn Monroe at the time of her death. We knew the address but did not have the name or phone number of the current owner. We simply arrived there and hoped for the best. I needed Barry Norman to film a piece-to-camera in front of the house, so permission to do so was vital. The owner came out when he saw us arrive. He was used to fans visiting the 'shrine' but this time there was TV equipment. This was May 1979. When I told him we were from the BBC in the UK he replied gruffly, *I don't think I should let you film here after what happened in your country last night, electing that dreadful woman as Prime Minister.* I did not know there were any socialists living in California!

Eventually he relented and I took a peak inside the spacious living room of Monroe's unpretentious house with the mandatory swimming pool beyond. In the garden there were some lovely, large flower pots bedecked with small shrubs, red geraniums and other bedding plants which made a good display. They helped form a perfect backdrop for Barry's piece to camera, except for one thing - the owner's car. I approached him gingerly to ask him to move it out of shot, to which he agreed rather reluctantly. He backed his gleaming black Cadillac and promptly knocked over half his display of pots. He fumed and cursed but we got our shot. After the filming I thanked him warmly without offering him even a dollar in compensation for his time and trouble. He deserved better.

We drove along Wilshire Boulevard to the unprepossessing Westwood Village Cemetery where Marilyn Monroe is buried. I was very moved by this visit. In a west-facing wall was a large piece of white marble on which was engraved *Marilyn Monroe 1926 -1962*. It was one of a dozen or so crypts within the wall. On hers were four red roses placed there on the instructions of her second husband, the famous baseball player Joe di Maggio. I noticed the crypt beside her was empty - I wonder who is next to her now. Here Barry Norman recorded another piece-to-camera which proved difficult. One of Hollywood's greatest sex symbols is buried beside a busy thoroughfare. After several false starts, the task was completed.

The filming of Barry Norman's pieces-to-camera was stressful for us all, mostly for him. He and I would decide in advance which aspects of the particular movie star's life story would be more effective if spoken to camera, rather than narrated later as commentary back in London. It always surprised me how well those randomly chosen pieces-to-camera fitted in to the finished documentary - instinct triumphs.

I recall one piece-to-camera in the documentary on Jean Harlow. Barry explained why the 1930s blonde bombshell who had died tragically in 1937 at the age of 26, dyed her pubic hair blonde. He explained that she usually dressed in white and wore no underwear. Barry ended his piece with the words *so what else was a girl to do?*

Back in London in the cutting room I was stumped. This was not going to work. What material could I use to follow that comment? Then I remembered a film clip from her

1935 movie *Reckless* which I had prepared before the filming trip. Preceding the dance number from this film, I had accidentally recorded the dialogue leading into it. Sure enough Jean Harlow's words in the movie were *I've got no-one to blame but myself.* Perfect. And she was wearing a white dress. In the transmitted documentary it all worked smoothly. You'd have thought it had all been meticulously planned.

Just before filming those pieces-to-camera for *The Hollywood Greats,* Barry Norman became uptight. No prompt machine or cue cards were available so he learned them. This made me tense too. Normally the director stands beside the camera to see exactly what is being shot. From my experience as a TV presenter in Australia, I knew one could be distracted by someone standing there. To help Barry do his best, I would close my eyes and lower my head during filming. I saw nothing. Here was I, the director, supervising the filming of a piece-to-camera which millions would later watch, with my head bowed. It helped.

Barry got the reputation for being *one take Barry.* Consequently when he tried to live up to his own expectations but occasionally fluffed his lines or was interrupted by a helicopter flying overhead, he became unnecessarily livid with himself. He stomped and swore, then calmed down and tried again. It was a fascinating procedure. He turned the process into an art form.

We both enjoyed visiting Edward G. Robinson's house in North Robertson Drive, off Sunset Boulevard. He was the only movie star to buy a house, fill in its swimming pool and replace it with a European rose garden. Despite his gangster movie image in *Little Caesar, Barbary Coast* and *The Amazing Dr. Clitterhouse,* he was a cultured Romanian called Emanuel Goldenberg who had emigrated to New York with his parents and brother in 1902. When he started school there, the class for non-English speaking immigrants was full, so he was obliged to enrol in a normal class. Within a year he was speaking fluent English without a trace of a Romanian accent, whereas his brother in the other class retained an accent for the rest of his life. Without that twist of fate the career of Edward G. Robinson might have followed a different path.

He was also an art connoisseur and at the side of his house he had built a private art gallery. He genuinely loved his pictures, especially the French Impressionists. He had to sell many from his collection when his first wife divorced him but he still had a fine collection when his second wife, Jane, toured the gallery with me six years after his death.

The Los Angeles house I enjoyed visiting most was owned by the famous Hollywood costume designer Edith Head who had won Oscars for dressing Olivia de Havilland in *The Heiress*, Hedy Lamaar and Victor Mature in *Samson and Delilah* and Elizabeth Taylor in *A Place in the Sun*. The site was up a hill off Laurel Canyon. It had a long, wide veranda down one side which was decorated in Mexican style, a mixture of bright and subdued colours, wooden and leather furniture, patterned cushions, exotic vases, gourds and decorative boxes. It was cool and relaxing, not what you'd expect to find in the home of a petite, black-fringed, well groomed old lady with glasses. What's more, she retained a keen sense of humour despite having to look after her ill, house-bound husband. Edith told us how Marilyn Monroe had liked the decor so much that she sent a van to Mexico to furnish her new Brentwood place in a similar style.

For the documentary about Hollywood itself, I needed to get shots of all the major studios. Because of the strict trade union laws at 20th Century Fox, Universal, Paramount, Columbia, MGM and Warner Bros., it was impossible to take a British film crew inside without having to pay an American union crew, which I had been forced to do earlier at the Astoria Studios in New York. I had an idea and it worked perfectly. I hired a helicopter for an hour so that my cameraman John Goodyer and I could film *all* the studios from the air. Using a zoom lens, we got some interesting material which was put to good use in the cutting room. The hire of the helicopter cost less than half the fee for an unwanted film crew.

We drove to Santa Barbara to film one of my favourite actresses from my teenage years, June Allyson - she with the dark blond bob and the husky voice, the girl-next- door with oomph. She had been a wonderful Jo in *Little Women,* a dutiful wife in *The Glenn Miller Story,* she had even sung *Thou Swell* in the Jerome Kern biopic *Words and Music* and here was I, in 1979, visiting her home to meet her. How much would she have changed?

I knocked on the door. I was disappointed. In the distance, I saw a rather stout woman with a different hairstyle. I endeavoured not show my disdain at her altered appearance, it happens in all walks of life. She opened the door and simply said *Come inside.* Her voice was not as husky as I had remembered. She led me into the living room. She was the housekeeper.

In that spacious and comfortable corner of the house I was greeted by the real June Allyson. Her hair style was still the same, the voice was the same and she still had that cheeky grin. She was actually 62 but looked twenty years younger. She talked fondly of Richard which was how she referred to her late husband Dick Powell. They were married for 18 years until his death in 1963. She was an ardent Republican and there was a framed autographed photograph of her with Richard Nixon. She proudly announced that her daughter was working for the Party in Washington.

In the interview with Barry Norman, she expressed her love and admiration for her boss at MGM, Louis B. Mayer, one of the few who did. *Mayer was the only family I ever really had.....I never found him an ogre. I loved him, I truly did.* The next time I visited the USA I saw June Allyson on TV. She was advertising incontinence pads.

We made fifteen *Hollywood Greats* documentaries in three years. They had been an enormous success and it was time to stop. Later production teams made *The British Greats* featuring Peter Finch, Gracie Fields, Jack Hawkins, Robert Donat and Leslie Howard. This series was equally popular. During this time, my connections with the film industry had enabled me to obtain film clips illustrating the careers of these performers at little or no cost. Then the movie studios were bought by oil magnates and cheese manufacturers who brought in financial advisors. The film companies started to ask thousands of dollars per minute, or part thereof for permission to use material from their vaults. My budget could not cope with such huge fees.

I looked elsewhere for subjects Barry Norman could tackle for his annual summer documentary series. An exception to this was when the team and I made *Ready When You Are. Mr. De Mille* for the centenary of the director's birth. It was produced in partnership with Paramount Pictures, who provided all film clips gratis in return for the right to screen it in the USA, Canada and Australasia.

Barry then turned his attention to a light-hearted look at various cities of the world - London, Chicago and Hong Kong. They too were successful. For one season he left his weekly film programme in order to host the regular BBC1 arts programme *Omnibus,* did not enjoy the experience, so I welcomed him back to the fold with open arms. In his absence we had, as guest presenters, the actress Maria Aitken, journalists Tina Brown and Miles Kington and TV presenter Glyn Worsnip. They were OK but Barry was king. He was a born presenter who loved movies and it showed.

In order to cushion the stark contrast between Barry Norman's presentation skills after the three new presenters, I commissioned Iain Johnstone, who had acted as stand-in several times for Barry, to prepare three ½ hour specials. He had already filmed a long and interesting interview with Jack Nicholson during his interminable stay in Britain as star of Stanley Kubrick's *The Shining*. Two more big stars were needed.

Iain and I knew Margaret Gardner, a former Hollywood press agent who now ran the London office of Rogers & Cowan, the American showbiz PR firm. She helped Iain arrange two studio interviews. The first was Candice Bergen, tall, elegant and beautiful who had graced the screen in the memorable Mike Nichols' movie *Carnal Knowledge* and had just made a romantic comedy with Jacqueline Bisset, directed by George Cukor (his last) called *Rich and Famous*. She had married quite late in life the French director, Louis Malle and had a European outlook on life, hardly Californian at all. She had a deep, luscious voice, no twang, was extremely articulate and had a marvellous sense of humour. I was besotted.

The other major star to get the TV special treatment was Paul Newman. His interview was recorded at BBC TV Centre one Saturday afternoon when the place was quiet. This suited him fine. He brought with him his wife, Joanne Woodward, a great actress who knitted non-stop in the green room whilst watching her husband on a monitor screen. She kept on mentioning under her breath in an admiring way, *those blue, blue eyes*. They had been married for nearly thirty years!

Paul Newman was by then 56 years old and still attractive, not as tall as I had thought, rather tired of movie-making but passionate about motor racing, a sport which worried his spouse. He had a laid-back quality, not unlike Clint Eastwood. He thought well and hard before he answered each question. This does not make scintillating television but with his good looks it did not matter too much. The Newmans were in London to sail along the Thames for a week in a hired canal boat.

The actor told me they would be collecting their daughter the next day at Teddington Lock. Can you imagine the scenario? A London family pulls up as usual at Teddington on their weekly outing. The wife notices the visiting barge and promptly says to her husband, *look at that chap over there, he's the spitting image of that movie star - the one in Butch Cassidy…you know…Paul Newman.* It would be the last place on earth you would expect to find the star himself.

Barry's return to the critic's chair was sensational. I was relieved. His replacements had been acceptable but nothing more. He was glad to be back and realised that this was what he wanted to do. From then on his career and weekly pay packet went into overdrive. However, against my wishes Barry was commissioned to make more *Hollywood Greats.* Production costs for this genre of documentary were now so prohibitive that only three were made one year, including Bing Crosby and two the next, Henry Fonda and John Wayne. The whole project then fizzled, just what I did not want to happen. It was a sad ending to a fine series. It reminded me of an episode in my personal life several years earlier.

My son had appeared in his primary school's production of *Joseph and his Amazing Technicolor Dreamcoat.* After singing his solo in Elvis Presley mode, the audience went wild. He was forced to repeat it. Still the applause was deafening. Later that evening he confessed, *Dad, I wanted to do it a third time.*

Dugald, I said, <u>*never*</u> *do it a third time.*

Nineteen   Executive Stress

In 1979 I became an Executive Producer which widened my brief. Although still in charge of Barry Norman's film programmes, I had other considerations. No longer responsible for the day-to-day production process, I could fight to get finance for projects, I could counsel and advise harassed producers, reminding them that *it's only television!* As a result, I developed neuritis, my nerve ends tingling down my buttocks and right leg. *You're usually very healthy, Barry,* said a colleague, *what's brought this on?*

Delegating, I replied. It did not last long, the neuritis, that is. Once you get used to it, delegating is the best way to work. The most frightening thing to learn is that nobody works the same way as you - and sometimes they do it better. Once you come to terms with that situation, life can only get better. I feel sorry for 'control freaks' these days even though I was probably one myself.

I remember being devastated during the editing of Barry Norman's Hong Kong documentary. The film editor turned to me and said *Oh, Barry you are relentless.* Here was I, sitting in the cutting room the whole time trying to be helpful and staying ahead of the game. Then I was accused of doing just the opposite. I went back to my office quite upset and relayed to one of my production colleagues that my film editor had called me *'relentless'*. His cool reply was, *well, you are*. It is hard to see yourself as others see you and I was learning fast.

One of my favourite pastimes as Executive Producer was to visit the set of the late-night chat show *Friday Night, Saturday Morning* at the then Greenwood Studio which was part of Guy's Hospital in central London. I knew the line-up of guest presenters, interviewees and music content in advance, but the producers were so competent there was little for me to do. I usually turned up after rehearsal just in time to eat a light supper with the guests. It may not seem like a job, but it is.

Between rehearsal and recording, the producer has a million things to check so I would chat to the guests to try to put them more at ease before their 'ordeal' as many regarded it. Some were not the remotest bit interested in my presence, like the poet Stephen Spender, the politician Joe Grimond, or the author Nigel Nicholson so I quickly left.

Others like *Starsky and Hutch's* David Soul; classical pianist John Lill, and comedienne Tracy Ullman were more amenable and pleasant. There were guest presenters, too, former Prime Minister Harold Wilson being the worst ever. My job often entailed escorting their partners to a reserved seat in the auditorium for the recording. Because the show needed an audience, it was recorded at around 8pm for transmission later the same evening at around 11.30pm. There was rarely time for editing; what was recorded was what was transmitted. For a guest presenter this was quite nerve-wracking.

Terry Jones, one of the *Monty Python* team, was so worked up that he had forgotten to bring black shoes to complement the suit he was wearing. I offered mine. I felt such a fool walking through the audience with Mrs. Jones in my grey suit with matching grey socks and no shoes!

Friday Night, Saturday Morning was the show where a young and nervous Victoria Wood made an early TV appearance; where the black American writer, James Baldwin, when asked by the guest presenter, Frank Delaney, how he felt arriving in Paris as a young, black homosexual man, replied, *I thought I was in heaven;* where the sedate Kitty Muggeridge was the only person in the audience yelling support for her husband, Malcolm, as he denounced Terry Jones for directing such a blasphemous movie as *The Life of Brian*. It was a lively programme, once again devised by my friend Iain Johnstone, who, true to form, departed after the first series when boredom set in. Frances Whitaker took over, which stood her in good stead for her later role as producer of the thrice-weekly *Wogan* on BBC1.

Soon after, I was asked to take charge of a weekly programme about television, which the then Controller of BBC2, Brian Wenham, wanted for the autumn schedules. It was to be hosted by Ludovic Kennedy, a stalwart of the BBC's current affairs team, no longer needed in that area but still under contract. He became the ideal presenter and thought up its title *Did You See...?* The three dots before the question mark were crucial according to Ludo, as everyone affectionately called him. He was intelligent, charming, articulate, a true professional even though his dress sense was at times shambolic. He had a bigger build than I had expected. If you see someone on television, usually only from the waist up, why are you surprised to find them taller or shorter, bigger or smaller when you meet them?

I have pondered this over the years and have come to the conclusion that it has something to do with the size of one's head in relation to the width of one's shoulders. Any other theories would be welcome. Our subconscious mind must be hard at work, even when we watch TV.

I had worked out a running order for *Did You See...?* There would be a summary of the week's TV, with Ludo adding his personal comments, then there would a discussion of three programmes from the BBC and ITV schedules with carefully chosen guests, followed by a quiz about past TV, ending with either a location report of a TV series in production or a topical interview with a TV personality.

After years of political neutrality in BBC Current Affairs, Ludo at first needed reassurance that he could express whatever he felt about the TV programmes he had seen that week. He seemed liberated by this new task. The regular producer of *Did You See...?* was John Archer with Ann Freer as director.

For the quiz element of the show I had contracted Sue Peacock. She had recently appeared in the documentary *The Big Time* where she had been given the chance to be trained as a presenter on BBC1's early evening current affairs programme *Nationwide*. She was young and pretty, but needed lots of rehearsal and production notes in order to give a reasonable performance.

In Ludo's eyes she was still an amateur and, although too gentlemanly to be openly rude to her, I could see his resentment. The quiz provided light relief lightened by showing some wonderful old clips, including my favourite from the 'live' children's magazine *Blue Peter* when the young elephant from London Zoo disgraced himself on the studio floor then dragged his keeper through the horrible mess.

After six weeks we dropped Sue but the remaining format stayed intact for the rest of its long life, despite the fact that many BBC producers, incensed by the pounding some amateur critics gave their beloved productions, did all they could, behind the scenes, to have *Did You See...?* cancelled. They did not succeed. Brian Wenham was our champion and as Controller BBC2 he had the final say. It was reminiscent of *Late Night Line-Up* a decade earlier.

Maria Aitken I had loved as an actress. She was the best Elvira I had ever seen in the National Film Theatre's production of Noel Coward's *Blithe Spirit*. She was having trouble with her eyes which made it difficult for her to continue as a stage and film actress. Resourceful as ever, she turned her talents to writing and presenting TV programmes.

You need a patron in television. Brian Wenham became mine, Roger Laughton, down from Manchester as Head of the newly-formed Network Features Department, was hers. I was Roger's deputy and so was assigned to attend the Greenwood Studio again for the recording of one of Maria's shows which she had devised, called *Private Lives*. It was a simple premise. Two well known guests would bring to the studio their favourite mementoes and explain, with prompting from Maria, what they meant to them. Once again my job was to look after the guests before the recording began.

I was looking forward to meeting Princess Michael of Kent when she was one of the guests. I had attended an art gallery opening the previous year when she had made the welcoming speech. She was tall, beautiful, charming and elegantly groomed, more royal than the Royals, into which family she had married after her Roman Catholic first marriage had been annulled. At the studios she was equally elegant, this time in a green evening dress which emphasised her blonde hair and wide, pale eyes. She was Austrian born but had spent her teenage years in Australia, so I decided to make the latter country the initial topic of conversation. I told her I was Australian. *Yes, I have been there,* she barked. A sore point, I surmised. I remembered seeing a photograph in an Australian newspaper of the modest Sydney suburban house she had lived in. She needed no reminder of that residence now that she was a princess. I changed the subject.

As Freud had been born in Vienna, and as I had experienced and benefited from psychotherapy, I brought this topic into the conversation. She was more forthcoming. *When I was in Vienna, at a time when psychotherapy was rather fashionable, I tried it and was told I was anally retentive.* I could not believe my ears. I had known a princess for 15 minutes and she had told me that!

I realised during the recording of the programme that Princess Michael's main problem is that she is a bad show-off. Subsequently I always enjoyed seeing her on TV as a *Spitting Image* puppet with other members of the Royal Family and their comments each time before her imminent arrival, *don't mention the war.*

A TV series of which I am particularly proud, was never liked by the other BBC - the ones who mattered, that is. I was Executive Producer, with Chris Mohr as Producer of a series called *Motives*. Once again the premise was simple - to examine the motives and impulses which drive people to be famous. The Irish psychiatrist, Dr. Anthony Clare, was presenting an interesting series on Radio 4 called *In the Psychiatrist's Chair*. I was fascinated by his interviewing style which enabled the interviewee to reveal strengths and weaknesses in an open and frank way. Sometimes in life when we have a problem, we go round and round in circles thinking it through, trying to resolve the situation, usually without success. In psychotherapy you state your problem and start going round in circles yet again. Suddenly the therapist makes a pertinent comment from a different perspective which almost frightens you. For a moment you are angry with him/her for deflecting you from your cosy treadmill of thought. Slowly you realise that you are approaching your problem another way and start to think differently. It is a rewarding process which so many people choose to shun through ignorance or fear. I am glad I needed that input all those years ago. It is therefore understandable that I was keen to make a success of this series. It was time, in my opinion, for Dr. Clare to build a wider audience for his skills and have his own TV series.

The famous people featured on *Motives* were the singer and former teenage star Petula Clark; the Labour politician who had faked his own suicide, John Stonehouse; the footballer with an alcohol problem, George Best; and the founder and editor of the satirical magazine *Private Eye* Richard Ingrams. The programme's title sequence revealed an endless series of opening doors which I found most effective. The set comprised a simple, comfortable room with strong lighting focused on the interviewee. I had remembered broadcasting pioneer Sir Huw Wheldon's maxim, *avoid the obvious at your peril*. So the interviews were shot mostly in tight close-up, rather like John Freeman's ground-breaking *Face to Face* interview series during the early 1960s.

I was riveted by every conversation recorded by Dr. Clare except the one with Richard Ingrams. His stiff upper lip attitude and disdain for this branch of medicine precluded him from revealing anything more than he intended. There was no way Anthony Clare was going to extract more from him in a 40-minute session. He needed years of therapy. Looking at Richard Ingrams these days, if I pass him in the street or see him at a media reception or book launch, I see him as an old, troubled man. He would be the first to disagree with me.

During the interview with John Stonehouse, it became apparent that he refused to take responsibility for his actions which had caused enormous distress to his family and parliamentary colleagues. He was, after all, a government minister when he disappeared. He blamed his other persona, the demon sitting on his shoulder, for his misdemeanours. What a cop out! I was not surprised when he developed heart trouble after his second marriage and died relatively young.

George Best used his beguiling charm to deflect certain probing questions but freely admitted his weaknesses and sought to discover their cause. For all of them, fame or notoriety had not been sought and all of them dealt with it differently. Nevertheless, the demon drink and a subsequent liver transplant failed to save him.

To my mind the most troubled of all was Petula Clark. On the surface she was a true professional, aware of but frightened by her talent. She had not forgiven her father for forcing her career along the teenage path he chose for her, not allowing her to blossom as a woman. She revealed much about herself and obviously felt guilty about being a working mother to her three children. But she needed to sing to feel alive and to be her own person.

Motives was transmitted on BBC2 during the summer when the schedules were full of 'repeats'. As a result, it received plenty of press coverage, the viewing audience figures were reasonable if not earth-shattering. It was the BBC executives who failed to see its potential. I chose to open the series with the Petula Clark interview because it was the most revealing. After it was broadcast, I remember my executive colleagues saying it was a nice interview with a pleasant woman. Couldn't they see it was a gentle plea for help?

In the early 1980s the new Controller of BBC1, Alan Hart, wanted a six-week chat show for the summer and asked for some ideas. Out of it came a pilot programme called *Paul Gambuccini in the 21st Century* which I believed had great potential. Paul was an American Anglophile and radio disc jockey who I felt was ready for a TV career. Each week the programme would tackle one aspect of 20th century life and illustrate what it might be like in the next 100 years.

For the 'pilot' we chose 'Transport'. A professor of physics gave a wonderful demonstration of how the transport system would evolve. I remember him saying that because of advancements in computer technology, travel would become more reliable. Now that the 21st century has arrived, his forecast was spot on.

I also chose a popular singer/songwriter at that time, Hazel O'Connor, who had starred in the British film *Breaking Glass,* to write and perform a new song relevant to the chosen topic. What she wrote for the 'pilot' was unmemorable and I doubt if I would have kept her on for the series.

As it happened, Alan Hart did not enjoy the 'pilot' sufficiently to commission the series which disappointed me. It was a good idea not particularly well executed, but I could have made vast improvements given the chance. It was not to be.

A programme idea which *did* get the go-ahead from the BBC1 Controller was a 10-part weekly series called *Show Business.* I brought together radio DJ Mike Smith to host his first TV show and Anneka Rice in her first reporting job for the Beeb. The other reporter was ITV's Sally James, who had a penchant for claiming expenses for absolutely everything from a bus fare to a new pair of shoes. This might have been acceptable in commercial TV but was pushing it a bit at the Corporation. That's what happens when the contract you offer is not sufficiently specific. I learned a lesson from that experience.

As gossip columnist for the show, my producers chose Peter Noble, who had a similar weekly column in the trade paper *Screen International.* I thought he was too old at 65 to pop up in a programme filled with young talent. However the team argued their case and I relented, only to find his weekly contribution most refreshing. In the first programme, at his office desk surrounded by mess, he mentioned that he had had lunch with Anthony Andrews of *Brideshead Revisited* fame, and what did they talk about? Anthony Andrews. He was first to break the news here that Sylvester Stallone was to star in and direct *Rocky IV* for the unprecedented fee of twelve million dollars.

During my many trips to the USA, I had become enamoured of a daily magazine programme called *Entertainment Tonight*. It moved at a cracking pace with no item lasting more than a couple of minutes. It suited my temperament and I wanted to do an equally upbeat UK version. I acquired the rights to show selected extracts from the US edition. As a result viewers in this country were able to see such items as Barbra Streisand at the premiere of her new movie; Gloria Estefan launching her latest album; and Joan Collins and Linda Evans modelling *Dynasty* fashions for charity.

Local reporters covered such events as Liberace's birthday party in London hosted by his fans; the Bee Gees at their country estate in the Home Counties; George Segal making a spoof on Robin Hood at Pinewood Studios; and the West End opening of the Broadway musical *Little Shop of Horrors*. Television's then most glamorous star, Selina Scott, was interviewed at 4am in the taxi taking her to work on BBC's *Breakfast Time*; the parents of the latest pop phenomenon, Boy George, chatted endearingly in their ordinary suburban home about their son's childhood; and fashion designer Zandra Rhodes spoke at London's Fashion Week about her latest collection. Mike Smith even announced that the BBC was considering acquiring the old ATV studios at Borehamwood in order to produce a twice-weekly soap opera. That was two years before the birth of *Eastenders*. He was also the first to show the results of Hollywood actor Paul Newman's latest venture - he held up two bottles of his special vinaigrette, long before they were seen on UK supermarket shelves.

There was a wonderful mix of items from all areas of show business and I was very proud of my baby. The producers, Jane Lush, Alan Cassells, Charles Miller, Bruce Thompson and Peter Estall worked like Trojans.

My dream was to have a daily edition of *Show Business* with a weekend omnibus but it was not to be. A further series was never commissioned. According to my BBC bosses it was too hectic and too trite. Nothing was dealt with in any depth. That was precisely my intention. There are times when analysis is unnecessary particularly at 7pm on Friday evenings. To British TV executives magazine programmes about show business are not their cup of tea. It is the BBC's blind spot.

One of the producers of *Show Business,* Alan Cassells, came down from Leeds on a short term attachment. He was older than the rest of the team, more my own age, and I knew how difficult it must have been for him living in 'digs' in London away from his family. When I learned his wife was joining him one weekend, I invited them to my apartment for Sunday lunch. I decided against a roast dinner, instead I would make Hungarian goulash the previous night which would taste even better then next day. This was 1983 when supermarkets closed at 6pm on Saturdays and did not re-open until 9am Monday.

I bought all the ingredients that Saturday afternoon and started preparing the meal in the early evening. The phone rang while the goulash was simmering. It was an actress friend with yet another crisis in her life. I had assumed the role of her unofficial counsellor. Listen I did and listen some more.

Then I smelled my burnt goulash. I ended the conversation abruptly and proceeded to repair the damage as best I could. I chopped off the burnt edges of the expensive sliced, lean beef but the goulash sauce had a burnt taste. I had used up all my ingredients and could not start again.

At lunch the next day I announced that I was serving them a dish they had probably not tried before, smoked goulash. *Delicious*, they said.

Twenty   Go With The Flow

I was depressed about my career. I was 53 years old and had recently realised that everything I produced had a 'Barry Brown' look to it. I had established a production style which looked the same whatever the subject. This was my terrible secret and I was not going to reveal it to anyone.

Years earlier I had had another secret. Whenever I went filming I never shot exactly what I set out to do. It was a weakness I dared not admit. After all, everyone else knew exactly what they were doing, I could tell. Their films knitted together so beautifully. I had trouble making what *I* had shot look as if it had been intentional. With a bit of luck, I always managed to edit my film into shape but it was never perfect. Why couldn't I direct film like other people?

The BBC had many extra-curricular activities for its employees, one of which was the BBC Film Club. As well as screening and analysing current movies, the group financed a short films competition for its members. One year I was invited to be one of the judges, alongside Mike Wooller and Tony Palmer, both respected TV film-makers. About half way through the judging, Tony Palmer said quite casually *isn't it strange how you never end up filming what you intended to film.* I could not believe my ears. I wasn't a freak after all. It happens to everyone. The relief was immense. My secret was out but now I had another one.

By 1983 I realised that I would never make another documentary. It was time for younger people to step in and create their own style. I contemplated early retirement. My unofficial patron, Brian Wenham, now Director of Programmes had other plans. BBC TV had advertised for a Head of Purchased Programmes but no one had been appointed. This was the department which bought movies and TV series. I was offered the job. I was flattered. No formal interview would be necessary, just a private chat with the Controllers of BBC 1 and 2.

The Controller of BBC1 demurred so I had a second chat. I also had to meet my prospective new boss, Alan Howden, General Manager, Programme Acquisition - titles are very important at the BBC. All was rather amiable and after a slight hiccup and more negotiation, the job was mine. The BBC is full of tradition. When a senior executive is appointed, it is customary for the Director of Programmes to summon both channel Controllers for a congratulatory drink. Alan Howden was also present and they toasted my appointment with a tepid glass of white wine. Brian Wenham turned to Alan and said in my presence, *there Alan, here he is and you didn't want him in the first place.* I pretended not to hear.

I was now leaving TV production to others and so, just before my 54th birthday, I started my new job. I found it difficult. There was much to absorb and a staff of forty to get to know. The job entailed a weekly meeting with Controllers BBC1 & 2 to discuss what movies and TV series the department hoped to buy from UK and overseas.

I introduced an Attachment System whereby other BBC employees from other departments with a good movie and TV knowledge of films and TV series, would be trained on how to obtain broadcast quality material, check it for suitability and promote it. It is the only one noticeable change I made during my six year tenure.

In the film cutting rooms downstairs a film editor called Ken Locke became the department's "strong-language editor". In the Thatcher years in the UK, the transmission of four-letter words was a no-no. Many good movies, made to be shown in the cinema, contained these words. Some considerate directors made two versions during shooting. The strong language would be used for cinema; tamer words would be substituted for TV.

Airline versions of movies were too sanitised for a responsible organisation like the BBC to screen; that is why the task of removing four-letter words fell to Ken. He was ingenious. From the soundtrack he would take a word or syllable from another scene and use it to replace the offending word. If all else failed, he would hire actors and actresses to imitate the voices of, say, Dustin Hoffman or Meryl Streep and re-record a more appropriate word.

It was a ridiculous exercise but because of it Ken achieved playful notoriety in newspaper and magazine articles. Eventually, the viewers who watched these movies, which were always scheduled beyond the 9pm watershed, complained so much about the scheduling of edited movies that the process was virtually abandoned.

Christmas was a hectic time for the department because that is when hundreds of movies and bought-in TV Specials were shown on both channels. The BBC is alarmingly competitive at this time of year and jealously guards the proposed transmission schedule. They also plan their programme promotion slots so carefully that everything works like clockwork and merges seamlessly. The schedulers do all they can to prevent viewers getting bored and switching to ITV or Channel Four.

One year they became concerned at the length of closing credits on movies. Steven Spielberg had 4 ½ minutes of them at the end of *Indiana Jones and the Temple of Doom*. For the TV premiere of the Spielberg epic on Christmas Day our department was asked by the schedulers if we could shorten the credits to 2 ½ minutes. Consequently we speeded them up - for contractual reasons they could not be reduced. We dubbed on the closing music at the correct speed. It took up a lot of time and energy and I was pleased with our efforts.

Christmas Eve was traditionally a Corporation holiday, except for those who *had* to work. I was at home when the phone rang. The Queen's Christmas Broadcast, which preceded *Indiana Jones and the Temple of Doom*, was under-running. Would we reinstate the closing titles to their original length? Such are the vagaries of broadcasting.

I was always pleased when we went to Los Angeles on our annual buying trip for the latest US TV series. ITV and Channel Four would go at the same time, see the same material at different times, then all would bid for the best or most suitable series. The bidding was at times fierce. The big US distribution companies would always try to sell a package of products - they knew some new TV series would be winners, others losers in the US ratings war, so the negotiations rarely concentrated on the price of one 'hot' series, but the overall price of the package.

It was an exciting time and the only motto to adopt was *win some, lose some*. It amazed me how worked up some executives got when they lost a deal. Men like to negotiate and win, that is why women are more suited to this area of broadcasting and why more are now succeeding. It sometimes alarmed me, when all the hype was over, how little it really mattered whether BBC, ITV or Channel Four got the better series, apart from the big ones like *Dallas* and *Dynasty* - they had been bought for the BBC before my time. When ITV tried to poach *Dallas* all hell broke loose. One

ITV executive even lost his job. It was not the gentlemanly thing to do.

The BBC bought *Cagney and Lacey, Miami Vice* and *Moonlighting,* the latter featuring Bruce Willis in his first step up the ladder of success. ITV got *Murder She Wrote, L.A. Law* and *The Equaliser,* and Channel Four got *Hill Street Blues* and *Cheers.* I learned about negotiation from my boss, Alan Howden, who was brilliant at it but I could not emulate him. I had to do it my way. After TV production, this was a very different skill.

What pleased me most about these trips was the chance to visit all the great Hollywood studios. I had visited 20th Century Fox in 1975 for that screening of *Lucky Lady.* Years later, as we drove up to the main gate, the huge, exterior New York set built way back in 1969 for *Hello Dolly* was still there.

As I turned a corner a Fox man pointed out the office block which had become part of the decks for *The Poseidon Adventure.* Around the next corner he did not have to say a word. I knew. Still standing there was the house the studio head Darryl Zanuck had built for Shirley Temple fifty years ago. Now it was nothing more than an unimportant office for a minor executive.

At the screenings in the theatre across the road, I was intrigued by the 'pilot' of a series called *Cover Up* because it was set in Central America. Out of curiosity I put several questions about its production to 20th Century Fox's Head of International TV Distribution, who was on a salary of nearly half a million dollars a year plus perks. Each time I made a polite enquiry he had to phone through to his secretary to see if she could find the answer. It was embarrassing. I never asked again.

To sell a TV series it is best to know nothing. I learned this at ABC in New York where I was previewing two mini-series for possible purchase. I was introduced to their Vice-President of Sales for Latin America and asked him what he thought of the mini-series I had been pre-viewing in the next room. *Barry,* he replied, *how do you expect me to sell anything if I've seen it?*

Back in Los Angles, the BBC bought *Cover Up* but during the making of Episode 2, the male star, Jon-Erik Hexam, was fooling around off the set with his stunt gun. Unbeknown to him it was loaded with blank cartridges and he accidentally killed himself. He was replaced by Anthony Hamilton and the rapport between him and his leading lady, Jennifer O'Neill was never convincing. The BBC was stuck with the series but mercifully it only ran for 13 episodes and attracted a minor cult following.

We stayed at the Bel Air Hotel, a haven off Coldwater Canyon Rd, with tiny bridges over a stream inhabited by white swans with a pretty gazebo on the lawn nearby. Each morning we rose early and headed for the particular studio scheduled that day. Coffee, orange juice and Danish pastries were on hand. One morning at Disney Studios we were ushered in to a cold, dismal screening theatre that had not been refurbished since the 1940s, or so it seemed. And no breakfast was ready.

As we viewed each episode of their new show it seemed less and less funny. That was why the BBC decided not even to bid for *The Golden Girls*. Nothing should be viewed on an empty stomach. Another lesson I learned was *never see several episodes of a comedy series one after the other.* The viewer sees them weekly, sometimes daily, but rarely consecutively. Back home, *The Golden Girls* became my favourite show - on Channel Four.

In the mid 1980s, mini series were all the rage in the USA. Everyone was making them and they got longer and longer. All I know, from viewing hours and hours of them, a 4 hour mini-series would have been better as a 2 hour TV Movie, that an 8 hour mini-series would have been better at 4 hours, without exception. They were usually self indulgent and quite humourless.

Everyone got on the bandwagon and churned out mini-series after mini-series, using such veteran movie stars as Barbara Stanwyck, Jane Wyman, Charlton Heston, Sylvia Sidney, Robert Mitchum and Anthony Quinn. US distributors tried to charge TV networks around the world exorbitant prices per hour. It worked for a while then the rot set in.

The hype surrounding these overblown mini-series was stupendous and I benefited from such extravagances by being wined and dined at some of the world's finest restaurants. One evening in London when nouvelle cuisine was popular, 20th Century Fox executives invited Alan Howden and me to dinner at the Inn on the Park. A 1000 calorie dinner menu was available at a ridiculously high price, so I settled for that. The others followed suit.

Next day in the office I commented to Alan on our abstemious behaviour the previous evening. *I don't know about you,* he said, *but when I got home I had to have cheese and biscuits!* Shortly afterwards restaurants of the world changed their tune. No longer would expense account meals comprise one lamb cutlet on a swathe of carrot puree topped with a sprig of rosemary. Huge char-grilled T- Bone steaks beside a mountain of French fries with a dollop of mustard and grilled tomatoes became fashionable again.

I received a letter one day from a distributor called John Kelleher. It began *Dear Bryan Brown...* As a joke, I ended my written response with *by the way, I am not the distinguished actor but a mere Australian TV executive* and signed it *Barry Brown.*

I received a phone call almost immediately full of apologies and an invitation to lunch at *Pomme D'Amour,* a popular restaurant in Holland Park. I arrived a couple of minutes early and was taken to the table my host had booked. Shortly afterwards, a tall, well dressed gentleman arrived. I stood up to shake his hand, saying *John Kelleher?* His reply was, *no, I am the drinks waiter, would you like an aperitif?*

Not everything was bought from the USA. Increasingly, Australia and, to a lesser extent, Canada became a source of acquired material. Broadcasters cannot produce all their programme output. It would cost too much. When my former boss Roger Laughton became Head of Daytime TV, in order to create a competitive schedule for BBC1, he needed an Australian soap opera. He asked me to view several episodes of *Neighbours* of which I was most critical. As an expatriate Aussie, I judged programmes from my homeland too harshly. I thought the BBC should not buy it.

But, replied Roger, *I need an Australian 'soap' for daytime, to be shown twice a day, and ITV have all the others. 'Neighbours' is all that's available so we've got to buy it.* That is how this Australian soap became such a big hit in the UK. What I failed to realise was what I take for granted about Australian life is mesmerising for British viewers. Constant blue, sunny skies, spacious living, no class system to speak of, appeal to British viewers sitting at home, cold and cramped in the middle of winter.

A Canadian producer John McGreevy used the well known actor and raconteur, Peter Ustinov, to present a TV series called *Peter Ustinov's Russia*. Although a British citizen, he is of Russian descent, in fact he was conceived in St. Petersburg. The two men spent many months together in the Soviet Union filming Ustinov's impression of it. It was delightful and the BBC bought it.

My PR pal, Margaret Gardner, arranged a dinner in Peter Ustinov's honour at Mr. Chow's in Knightsbridge. I was looking forward to listening to him, interspersed with some delicious Chinese food and some good French wine. I was seated next to his wife, Helene, who, like any good wife who is used to hearing the same stories year after year, ignored him and chatted to me.

All through the meal I could hear snippets of hilarious anecdotes out of one ear whilst trying to look interested in the daily lifestyle of the Ustinov household as narrated by Mrs. Ustinov, who was French and *not* a born raconteur.

The next afternoon the Ustinovs turned up at a Wardour Street Preview Theatre for the Press Screening of the first two episodes of the six part series. Russian tea poured from a samovar and ethnic cakes were served to preserve the spirit of the series without having to resort to vodka which was 'expensive' in BBC publicity-speak!

Peter Ustinov and I had also attended a reception in his honour at the Canada House in Trafalgar Square and on the final night of his London stay, a dinner was given in his honour at the home of the Canadian Ambassador attended also by former British Prime Minister, Edward Heath and other dignitaries. How much all this boosted BBC2's ratings for the Canadian-made series *Peter Ustinov's Russia* I do not know, but I enjoyed myself enormously.

At the end of the evening Peter gave me his latest book *Ustinov in Russia,* based on his TV series. As well as writing it, he had done all the drawings and taken most of the photographs which were superb. When I got home I opened it and read this inscription: *For Barry Brown - With thanks for your happy initiative and great kindness. Peter Ustinov.* Now that's what's I call a gentleman, an Englishman to a tee.

TV Markets where international buyers and sellers of feature films, TV movies, series, documentaries and 'specials' meet to party and do business, are held throughout the year at several venues. My favourite was Monte Carlo. Because I get car sick and cannot cope with the winding Grande Corniche from Nice to Monte Carlo in the back of a hire car, I used to hop in a helicopter for an 8 minute flight past the magnificent homes and swimming pools on the French Riviera to Monaco. It was a memorable trip and I looked forward to it every year.

The market was held at Loew's modern hotel built on reclaimed land, just down the road from the elegant Hotel de Paris, L' Hermitage Hotel and the Casino. Whenever I walked along the streets of this elegant yet sterile town with the pink Palace on the opposite hilltop, I had to remind myself how privileged I was to visit such a place, not as a tourist but as part of a day's work.

The Market itself reminded me of the brothels of Amsterdam where ladies of the night sit in dimly-lit rooms at the front of their houses trying to entice punters to sample their wares and pay a hefty price for the privilege. The converted bedroom suites at Loew's were used by TV executives and sales people for the same purpose. They stood in the doorway doing all they could to invite you in to sample their wares - same idea, different town, different people, different price.

The American broadcaster NBC entertained their clients with a series of lunches every day of the market at the stylish Hotel de Paris. I always made a point of attending. The food was good and the company convivial. One year I received an invitation for a Monday lunch, but I was not due to arrive in Monte Carlo until Tuesday.

No problem, said my host Bernard Shaw, *come on Friday instead.* I had a busy time at screenings and meetings and, although due for NBC's pre-lunch drinks at 12.45pm, I did not arrive until 1.15pm. I hastened through the revolving doors of the Hotel, dashed up the elevator to the top floor, past the magnificent Grill Room to a Private Dining Room where I had been many times before. I was surprised to find that I was the only one there.

I reasoned that everyone else would also be busy on the final day of the market, including my hosts. So I waited. Soon a tall, imposing gentleman arrived who introduced himself as Head of TVE, Spain's equivalent of the BBC. Next came the head of ZDF, one of Germany's top TV channels. I was impressed. Obviously Friday was NBC's bigwig day and I was there by default.

I was in my element and chatted easily with everyone. I was introduced to the only woman present, Nadia Lacoste, Prince Rainier's Press Secretary. I reminded her of our previous correspondence regarding *The Hollywood Greats* interview by the now deceased Princess Grace all those years ago. Robin Scott, whom I had known when he was Controller BBC2, said *hello*, sipped his drink, chatted to the other dignitaries, then called me to one side.

I think you are at the wrong lunch, he said. Prince Rainier was due to arrive at any moment. I made my apologies, waited interminably for the elevator down to the hotel foyer where I was informed that the NBC party had been moved to the Ground Floor. A notice informing guests had been placed on an easel for everyone to see on arrival. Unfortunately, when I know where I'm going, there is no stopping me. I put on blinkers and head straight there.

On my return to London I relayed my dilemma to Michael Grade who was now Controller BBC1. He told me he had done the same thing at London's Café Royal. There were several reception rooms on the first floor, he went into the room at the top of the stairs, took a whisky from the waiter's tray, chatted to people he knew, was surprised to find so many politicians present, more surprised when dinner was announced. His invitation had stated a Cocktail Party. He quietly extricated himself and went to the correct function room next door.

Although I had made a decision never to attend the Cannes Film Festival again, I later visited the elegant French Riviera town itself several times for two of television's biggest markets - MIP-TV each April and MIPCOM every October. No market full of salesmen could function without buyers, so in order to ensure that there were plenty of the latter, the organisers provided buyers from the largest broadcast companies around the world with free accommodation, plus free limousine pickup from Nice Airport.

I either stayed the Carlton Hotel or the Martinez in a room with superb views of the Mediterranean Sea. It is easy to start taking this lifestyle for granted but I tried not to. When you are a buyer the whole world wants to contact you. I received at least 50 messages a day and countless invitations to parties. I ignored the former and accepted the latter - it was the only way to survive. I had arranged a full screening and meetings schedule before I left London - those who made the effort beforehand to contact me about their product and suggest a meeting time, deserved to be given priority. It also suited my preference for orderliness rather than the excitement of keeping one's options open.

These TV markets were amazing. As Michael Caine said all those years ago at the Film Festival, it would take one 10 months of constant travelling to see those one can make contact with in a few days at Cannes. I worked hard and I played hard. It took forever to walk along the Croisette, I knew nearly everyone and stopped for a chat. My fondest memories were the daily lunches on the private beaches. To sit in the spring and autumn sunshine with good company, attentive service and marvellous food, all financed by someone else's expense account, was bliss. The French make a fortune out of these events.

Every year the TV executives use Cannes to launch their new product with an influx of star names. At some lavish parties I remember meeting Patrick Stewart who was then starring as Captain Luc Picard in *Star Trek: The Next Generation;* the *Tom and Jerry* animators Hanna and Barbera; Chuck Jones and Fritz Freleng who created Bugs Bunny & Co.

These TV markets have their down side too. I always found it sad to see former high powered executives in their sixties, having been let go by their global corporations, unable to let go of the excitement and glamour of being someone special. They could not come to terms with the fact that they were no longer important. I vowed that when I turned sixty and retired from the BBC I would never set foot again at another TV Market or Film Festival and I never have.

Twenty One

Not Shy, but Retiring

A friend, a few years older than I once told me, *you'll be surprised who keeps in touch after you retire*. He was right. Just before my sixtieth birthday in early 1990, I attended some wonderful retirement parties. The American TV distributors gave me a lunch party at The Groucho Club, the famous media watering hole. The British distributors gave me a lunch party at the now defunct Museum of the Moving Image (MOMI). At the presentation I opened my gift of six crystal brandy glasses and in front of everyone dropped one and broke it. The BBC did me proud. I was guest of honour at a black-tie dinner in the Sixth Floor Suite, attended by close colleagues. My former boss, Will Wyatt, by now Deputy Managing Director, BBC TV made a funny speech reminding me of several instances in my career which I would rather forget, but everyone else laughed their heads off.

The following evening the Managing Director, Paul Fox hosted a drinks party for 200 which included the whole of the Programme Acquistion Department, former colleagues from other areas of the BBC, and London-based TV distributors. I was elated, not at all sad at the prospect of ending my 23 years at the Corporation. Overall I had had a very happy time with constant job satisfaction, which few of my contemporaries outside the media could claim. It was time to go.

Admittedly I was setting up my own business *Barry Brown Broadcasting* (aka BB3) and would work from home as a consultant. It was a way of settling slowly into retirement. Before that I went on a luxury seven week air trip around the world with my then partner. In fact we celebrated my 60th birthday in Australia with my 84 year old father. He once told me *Barry, you can never have enough money in retirement*. Having seen others unable to retire because they needed more and more capital behind them to ensure their financial security in old age, I decided I would have to make do with what I had. I was aware that all my dreams stopped here. What I now owned was 'it', except for my lump-sum retirement package, my BBC pension and the £300 my great aunt in Blackpool had bequeathed me.

My consultancy flourished for a few years. I had several clients, including the BBC, whose exclusivity clause forbade me from accepting work from ITV and BSkyB. What I learned from being a media consultant is that very little of the expensive advice you give is ever acknowledged, let alone implemented. Anything you achieve is minimal.

One company put me under contract then kept me away from the TV production side of their business, the area in which I was most proficient. My task instead was to offer new ideas for future production. Not one of them came to fruition. The company went bust before they could implement any plans for expansion. One of my ideas was to acquire the TV movie rights to the American singer Peggy Lee's autobiography *Miss Peggy Lee*. A fee for the rights was negotiated. I flew to Los Angeles and visited the 70 year old bedridden singer in her Bel Air mansion for a week and discussing with her how to dramatise various elements of her life and which actress might best portray her. She had a sweet-nature and a good sense of humour but a lifetime in the music business had made her mistrustful. At the time she was suing the Disney Corporation for fees due to her for the video release of their animation classic *The Lady and the Tramp*. Not only had she recorded several of the voices but had written and sung many of the songs in the movie. She won eventually but her legal costs were astronomical. She acted on her principles and ended up with virtually nothing. Potential litigants take note. It is ironic that one of her best known hits is the song *Is That All There Is?*

Peggy Lee's home was subtly furnished in provincial French style with good furniture and lots of pink drapes and cushions, all plain - no checks or patterns anywhere. Understatement has always been Peggy Lee's trademark. She was most hospitable, her West Indian housekeeper providing meals on a tray and endless cups of tea, made on Miss Lee's insistence the proper way - in a teapot and served in bone china cups and saucers, a rare phenomenon in the Californian tea-bag-in-a-glass culture.

It was here that I first sampled grilled swordfish and tofu ice cream. Peggy Lee and I got on extremely well but at times the whole situation reminded me of the Billy Wilder movie *Sunset Boulevard*. One day her Mexican handyman rummaged through the loft in her three-car garage, set up a 16mm projector in her bedroom and loaded an inflammable roll of old film. Peggy and I watched together this 1950s documentary about her preparation and recording of a new album for release while her 'servant' stood silently by the projector, adjusting the focus unnecessarily.

It showed the young Peggy Lee as a top notch musician wholly in charge of proceedings and knowing exactly what she wanted to achieve musically. She was a strong lady who had married the now deceased alcoholic guitarist, Dave Barber and had produced a daughter and a couple of grandchildren. After the documentary screening, elements of which we hoped to include in the teleplay, I tried to suggest to the singer that she could have the film transferred to videocassette at little cost, for safety as well as practical reasons but she was not interested - just like Norma Desmond in the movie. She had the occasional visitor - the jazz critic from the *Los Angeles Times*, Leonard Feather and his wife and the larger-than-life comic actor Dom De Luise, but, apart from inviting a hairdresser, who used to tour with her, to provide me with reminiscences of that era, her staff were her main company.

She lived like a recluse with her beloved cat *Baby*. Peggy Lee was right to be mistrustful. I learned later that the company who had sent me there did not even have enough money in the bank to pay a deposit on the acquired rights. It was an embarrassment to me but Peggy understood that it was not my fault and we remained friends. Soon after, my services as a consultant for that company were terminated, just before it went bust.

At the BBC I had built up a friendship with Robert (Bob) Kingston, a music publisher and film distributor who had sold Channel Four six movies starring the *world's first singing cowboy* Gene Autry. I realised that no-one under 50 outside the USA knew who Gene Autry was, so I suggested an introductory ½ hour programme called *Back in the Saddle Again - the Making of A Gene Autry Western*. Through his contacts with Gene Autry's right-hand man in California, Bob ensured that extracts from his 93 movies would be made available at a reasonable price. That is how Bob and I came to co-produce this commissioned compilation programme for Channel Four.

Our aim was to explain who Gene Autry was, how he got into movies, what kind of movies he made and how they were made. I was thrilled to be back in programme-making. I no longer cared if it had a 'Barry Brown' look to it which had so obsessed me ten years earlier. I loved deploying the new video editing techniques which had emerged. Channel Four gave us the money to make the programme and make it we did retaining all overseas TV and video rights.

The programme was sold to the USA and Canada, to Poland, Russia and Australian pay TV, but nowhere else. Buyers these days are usually under 50. They neither know nor care about an old Hollywood cowboy legend, yet in the 1940s he was a top box-office star in Hollywood. When the programme was shown early one September morning on Channel Four only a few hundred thousand tuned in and I can guess their ages. The important thing is that Bob and I are still the best of friends.

Five years after my official BBC retirement, work was drying up. At 65 I was now an orphan and aware of my own mortality, so I had one last stab at production. With the help of my friends at Limitless Communications I wrote and produced a 60 minute video narrated by actor Roy Hudd called *Stars of Victory*. It comprised extracts from British wartime movies made between 1942 and 1945 which featured well known music hall and variety stars of the day - singer Donald Peers; comediennes Elsie and Doris Waters (known as 'Gert and Daisy'); the incomparable performer Sir George Robey; duo pianists Rawicz and Landauer; and the husband-and-wife singing team of Anne Ziegler and Webster Booth, among others. It was produced to coincide with the 50th Anniversary of VE and VJ Days and once again I enjoyed the many, many hours I spent working on it. As I mentioned earlier, once you learn to ride a bike, you never forget. The same goes for producing radio and TV programmes. Producing a programme is like giving a dinner party - you have certain ingredients, certain facilities, a certain amount of time to do it in, and it's got to be a good show. *Stars of Victory* sold reasonably well considering the plethora or specialist videos on sale in celebration of these two historic events. Money was not the issue. I wanted to make it and I did. As long as I did not lose money on the venture I was happy. And I didn't.

My BBC consultancy contract which had started on 1 March 1990 ended on 30 September 1995. I decided to call it quits and *Barry Brown Broadcasting* was no more and I had no more links with the BBC after 28 years. I stopped reading the trade papers and began my full retirement in earnest. It was not difficult. I still had many friends within the media with whom to keep in touch.

I now lived alone in a large flat in central London filled with clutter and memorabilia collected during 30 years in the UK. I once asked a friend why she still kept her mother's unused underwear when she had been dead for 25 years. *Because I have the room,* was her reply. I made a decision to live somewhere smaller. I feel liberated by downsizing to a small flat in a large apartment building with elevators and a supermarket below. My friend, Betty Leese, lent me a book called *Clutter's Last Stand* and from it I learned how to get rid of accumulated mess. I am forever grateful to her.

Every now and then I reminisce with friends about my career and also lecture on cruise ships about the *stars in my eyes.*

I learned a long time ago that you have to get life right for you - no-one does it for you. What I found more difficult to accept was that life is unfair. Despite the many problems and heartaches I have had to face in eighty years of life, I am at peace and content with myself. I no longer have to say, *this and better will do me!*

Index

L

Lake, Alan 63
Lamaar, Hedy 206
Larry, Sheldon 79, 83
Laughton, Charles 200
Laughton, Roger 215, 229
Laye, Evelyn 24
Lean, David 70, 71, 72, 75, 76, 77, 91, 131, 132
Lee, Peggy 236, 237, 238
Leese, Betty 240
Lehrer, Tom 35
Leigh, Janet 66
Leigh, Vivien 29, 58
Lemmon, Jack 170, 171
Leroy, Mervyn 196
Lester, Richard 163, 164
Lewis, Geoffrey 188
Lewis, Jerry 151
Liberace 220
Lindfors, Viveca 52, 53
Lindsay, Judy 193, 194
Lisi, Virna 91, 92
Locke, Ken 224
Locke, Sondra 183, 186, 189
Logan, Joshua 122
Lollobrigida, Gina 92, 93
Lombard, Carole 197
Loren, Sophia 89, 93, 94, 95, 96, 157, 158
Losey, Joseph 81, 107
Loy, Myrna 12
Lumet, Sidney 172
Lumley, Joanna 88
Lush, Jane 220
Lynn, Vera (Dame) 110

M

MacDonald, Jeanette 21
MacGraw, Ali 172
MacLaine, Shirley 63, 66, 169
Magee, Patrick 131
Makeba, Miriam 54
Mallinson, Sue 200
Mamoulian, Rouben 144
Mancini, Henry 157
Mankiewicz, Joseph L. 100, 101, 103
Marcos, Ferdinand & Imelda 117, 118, 119
Markova, Alicia (Dame) 177
Marriott, Steve 39
Martin, Tony 177
Marx, Barbara 201
Marx, Groucho 201
Marx, Zeppo 201
Mastroianni, Marcello 91, 92
Matthau, Walter 187
Mature, Victor 206
Mayer, Louis B. 13, 207
McCambridge, Mercedes 169
McCrea, Joel 199, 200
McDowell, Malcolm 130
McGreevy, John 229
McKern, Leo 70
Medina, Patricia 62
Melnick, Daniel 175
Mercer, Jane 148, 149
Mercouri, Merlina 63
Miles, Sarah 70, 74, 75, 82
Miller, Charles 220

Shaffer, Anthony & Peter
101
Sharp, Margaret **194**
Shaw, Bernard **231**
Shearer, Moira **177**
Sheffield, Johnny **16**
Sidney, Sylvia **228**
Simmons, Jean **128**
Simpson, O.J. **157**
Sinatra, Frank **35, 201**
Singer, Aubrey **148, 150**
Skolimowski, Jerzy **92**
Smith, Delia **55**
Snowdon, Lord **88**
Soul, David **212**
Spender, Stephen (Sir) **212**
Spiegel, Sam **11**
Spielberg, Steven **169, 189, 225**
Spigelgass, Leonard **198**
Stallone, Sylvester **219**
Standing, John **168**
Stanwyck, Barbara **99, 228**
Steel, David MP **45**
Stern, Isaac **34, 35**
Stewart, Patrick **233**
Stonehouse, John MP **217**
Strasberg, Lee **158**
Strauss, Helen **124**
Stravinsky, Igor **35**
Streep, Meryl **224**
Streisand, Barbra **220**
Subotstsky, Milton **131**
Sutherland, Donald **106**
Sutherland, Joan **35**
Swanson, Gloria **144**
Syms, Sylvia **131**

T

Taylor, Billy **152**
Taylor, Elizabeth (Dame)
31, 58, 84, 126, 157, 165, 206
Temple, Shirley **12, 21, 226**
Thompson, Bruce **220**
Thorndike, Sybil (Dame)
29, 30
Tidmarsh, John **49**
Tiomkin, Dimitri **145**
Todd, Ann **76**
Todd, Richard **131**
Tracy, Spencer **13, 194, 195**
Trevelyan Oman, Julia **129**
Trinder, Tommy **24**
Tushingham, Rita **164, 165, 200**
Tyler Moore, Mary **174**

U

Ullman, Tracy **212**
Unsworth, Geoffrey **125**
Urban, Harry, Stuart, Mark
107, 108
Ustinov, Peter **87, 117, 229, 230**

V

Van Peebles, Mario **188**
Vaughan, Robert **129**
Visconti, Luchino **36, 79, 80, 81, 83, 85**

W

Walker, Alexander **119**
Wallace, Jean **19**
Walter, Jessica **188**
Walton, Emma **156**
Ward Baker, Roy **131**
Waters, Ethel & Doris **239**
Wayne, John **145, 210**
Weissmuller, Johnny **16, 175**
Welles, Orson **9, 10, 62**
Wenham, Brian **10, 213, 214, 215, 223**
Wheldon, Huw (Sir) **115, 217**
Whitaker **188**
Whitaker, Frances **213**
White, Betty **55**
Whiting, Leonard **84**
Wilde, Cornel **19, 20**
Wilder, Billy **99, 237**
Wilder, Gene **160**
Wilson, Harold MP **212**
Winger, Debra **168**
Winner, Michael **74, 91, 92, 162**
Withers, Jane **12**
Wogan, Terry **15**
Wood, Natalie **195**
Wood, Victoria **213**
Woodward, Joanne **209**
Wooller, Mike **222**
Wyatt, Will **235**
Wyman, Jane **228**
Wynter, Mark **39**
Wynyard, Diana **29**

Y

Yentob, Alan **10**
Young, Freddie **71, 75, 76, 77**
Young, Loretta **34**

Z

Zadora, Pia **118**
Zanuck, Darryl **226**
Zeffirelli, Franco **79, 84**
Ziegler, Anne & Booth, Webster **239**

Lightning Source UK Ltd.
Milton Keynes UK
15 January 2010

148633UK00001BA/9/P